Puck and Minnie

All That Is

Suzanne J. Warfield

ISBN: 1545157308
ISBN 13: 9781545157305

To my friend and editor, Robert Bacon, who has so much faith in my writing and me, I dedicate this book with the deepest gratitude.

1

I was barking. I remember that. Barking and barking, just in a lazy way. I like to hear my own voice . . . and it gets lonely very early in the morning. We bark to let others of our species know where we are and what's going on. In my case, I was just making anyone who happened to be listening aware that I was bored. Many centuries ago, we always expected an answer. Different packs, living some distance away, would bark or howl back that they had made a kill that day and now they were full and sleepy. Others would howl news of one of us dying or yip with excitement over a recent new litter. Some would just honor Grandmother Moon, or express how good the cold air felt in their nostrils, or how thankful they were to All That Is for their time here, serving The Earth Mother. But that was before, when all of my kind served the Earth Mother and not Hu-mans. After that change, things got really hard and lessons became confusing. Early Hu-mans could hear us and know us, but now Hu-mans have refused to learn our language. Humans quiet us. They like to think they control us. So, we speak less.

Scarcely anyone answers anymore. Rarely do I hear a complete conversation. Mostly, what comes back to me is a fragment. Those who are listening often respond with just a one-word question, such as "What?"

or "Who?" It's almost as if they have forgotten how Dog communicates. Well . . . sadly, if the truth be told, most have forgotten.

We essentially lost our voices over time, and our memories too, but we always know our purpose. Always. From the moment we are created out of Divine thought, it's inscribed on our Souls to Teach, Honor and Love. But all three commandments are complicated. Hu-mans are difficult to teach because the species doesn't listen to hear. Hu-mans are, for the most part, not honorable. And the love they think and feel isn't the same we know. Overseeing our Hu-man is a difficult mission.

Thankfully, we get to go Home in a blink of time. Some of us sooner than others, but the lessons are always taught and, yes, learned. Whether we leave this earthly place we call The Earth Mother as newborns or are lifted from a Hu-man's loving heart at an age of fifteen or so earth years, we go Home only when a part of our mission is completed. Even those of my kind who suffer at the hands of a low-level Hu-man and are sent Home through violence and pain know their worth cannot be diminished. Those canines are the most grateful to arrive at The Bridge. We, who are already Here, celebrate their return. Their passage has been profound, because the lessons of Kindness and Forgiveness are the most needed to be learned by all those who are new to Life as a sacred journey. We choose our Hu-man, and we go back into each Life as many times as it takes for that person to become one with our God, whom we know as All That Is. And the Most High, All That Is, resides in everything; in us, in them, and in all the particles that make up Earth.

Those Hu-mans who ignore The Earth Mother survive on the most basic level of existence. They are motivated mostly by fear and ego. They believe that they *are* the bodies of Life and nothing else. What they don't understand, they fear and kill. What confuses them enrages their egos. These Hu-mans believe themselves to be all-powerful and in control, but they are fools. They are the hardest to teach and nurture, but over time the purity of our Hearts wins over theirs, even though it will take many, many visits back to Earth School, as we refer to it.

Sometimes, a fur Soul who has endured a passing of a difficult nature comes back to us exhausted, but not for long. Francis, The Holy One,

gathers us around him and holds the newly arrived Hu-man-abused fur
Soul next to his chest and recites what we have all heard so many times
before. He once repeated this same speech as a prayer for Hu-mans when
he visited Earth, but in reality his words are an instructional reminder
for our species alone. It is Dog law, and All That Is has made us an instrument of Peace to teach the following:

> Where there is hatred, we sow love;
> Where there is injury, pardon;
> Where there is doubt, faith;
> Where there is despair, hope;
> Where there is darkness, light;
> Where there is sadness, joy.
> We ask that we always be reminded not to seek what we give;
> To console as to be consoled;
> To understand as to be understood;
> To love as to be loved;
> For it is in giving that we receive;
> It is in pardoning that we are pardoned;
> It is in dying that we are born to eternal Love.

This is all we know. This is who we are. This is why Dog comes into
Hu-man lives; to do as we are instructed. We teach Hu-mans to live in
the moment with unconditional Love. We reappear over and over with
the same message. We come Home, rest, and then continue back to The
Earth Mother to keep teaching. Most of the time we stay with our chosen
Hu-man. Only those Hu-mans who completely learn may become one
with All That Is and extend their perfect Hearts to help others. We're
overjoyed when they cross The Bridge with us. We love them so.

But, alas, now back to me. There I was, engrossed in my barking as
I described earlier. I really don't remember exactly what happened, only
that a presence was behind me before I could identify that it was a man
of the Hu-man species, big and rough. He grabbed me and unfastened
the lead that kept me tied on my Hu-man's porch. I do recall he had a

familiar scent about him, a sour stench that had always made my eyes water and stirred faraway memories of other Lifetimes.

I knew this heinous entity was of importance because of my past reincarnations, but his current significance was vague, his image coming and going like mist in an uneven breeze. I remember his name sounded something like . . . Hayes. Unfortunately, that name and I have a dark history together. Our Dog names change from Lifetime to Lifetime, even our gender on occasion, but we never forget the events that must be healed and balanced before we can move on and ultimately into The State of Grace. Yes, I have it now. This Hu-man, Hayes, was the one who took my Life before, as he had done in so many of my reincarnations. There are too many of my Dog iterations to list here, but during this narrative I'll tell you about the Lifetimes that are the most important to me. And of course I'll tell you about Minnie.

I hear, "Hello, sleepyhead." The voice is above me, and I roll my head over on my Angel's lap to gaze up at her as she smiles back at me. "You've been asleep since you arrived! You missed your party."

I close my eyes and stretch my paws, the scent of rich grass filling my senses. Warm sunlight brings new Life into my body. I open my eyes as a white feather drifts down from my Angel's wing and settles on my nose. I am surely Home. There is no describing the Bliss that I and the other canines experience upon returning Home, to this place across The Bridge that separates Here from There.

"Are you ready to know what happened?" the golden voice asks. "Or do you need more time to adjust?"

I roll away and try to stand, but I feel a bit shaky and just sit up instead. I look at my Angel, whose name is Azul, and wag my tail. I so love my Angel. "I missed you," I say, letting my jaw fall open into a sloppy smile.

"You know that I'm always with you," Azul says softly.

"Yes, but I wish you were really there with me, with a Hu-man body and stuff. I've met some Angels on Earth who have taken Hu-man form. They shine so brightly! They're everywhere on Earth. Hu-mans don't see them, but we do. I wish you would come—"

Azul runs a hand over my head and laughs, stopping me. "Then who would be here to welcome you Home?"

I pounce up into Azul's lap and cover her glowing face with what would be wet kisses on Earth. Here, however, our kisses aren't slobbery. To this point, we now have light bodies that look something like the form we assumed when on Earth, but that's about it. Our biggest problem is deciding what image of Dog to take, as so many breeds exist.

Azul laughs and hugs me. She looks into my eyes, smiling all the while. "Come now, Puck, we have work to do. You must be told what happened that caused you to suddenly come Home, and we have to plan your next journey. I blessedly lifted from you the memory of pain and anguish, but there are wrongs to be righted."

"I'm ready, Azul. But first, please tell me if Minnie is all right. I must know that."

"Your Minnie is fine, Puck, but she remains very sad over losing you. She has no knowledge of what happened, only that you vanished from her porch while she slept that night. She cries every day and has exhausted the nights looking for you. After our talk, you have permission to go and be with her. She won't be able to see you, but she will feel you next to her on the porch. She will talk to you and perhaps cry a bit more. No matter, your presence will comfort her tonight. Then you must come back to me, and we'll plan your next visit to Hu-mans."

"Thank you, Azul. She's almost There—or should I say Here! She's learned much after so many times on Earth."

"Yes, Puck. And so have you. But there's still much work to be done. Especially concerning the troubled Soul of the Hu-man who caused your death and spreads so much sorrow on Earth. He continues to be your mortal enemy because of your actions at the start of your relationship with Minnie." Azul's eyes pierced mine. "You have no one but yourself to blame, Puck. Some lessons are harder to learn—and teach—than others. But I have faith in you."

"Oh, Azul, this Hu-man called Hayes is a bad man. He's the one who stole me off Minnie's porch and caused my death, sending me Home this time, isn't he? How can I teach Love to someone like that?"

"Through true Forgiveness. Not only toward him but toward your-self as well. Love heals everything"

"I can't forgive something I don't understand," I said, pouting.

"Ah, but you will understand, Puck. Very soon there will be a Lifetime that will make anger and hatred painfully clear to you. Just remember that I'm always with you, dear Heart, and that time on Earth is just a blink of an eye to those of us who are Here but seems to be quite long to Hu-mans. Now, let's review by going back to the very beginning. As I recall, you were . . ."

2

The night storm came quickly and took the village by surprise. The Hu-man Mia sought frantically for fingerholds and toe-holds in the slippery rock wall. The angry floodwaters snapped at her lower legs like a pack of hungry wolves. She could only hope that her family had escaped through the mountain pass and reached higher ground. She would have fled with them had it not been for the panic of waking and not finding her three-year-old daughter, Suta, sleeping close beside her. In those precious moments before the waters came, Mia found Suta outside their hut, relieving herself.

Because of the fear of predators, the child was never to leave the hut for any reason without her mother. However, in the youngster's mind this wasn't an issue, as her need would take only the briefest time. What could happen? By the time Mia snatched up her daughter in her arms, the floodwaters had roared into their area, cutting them both off from the mountain pass and leaving no choice—if they were to survive—but to scale the sheer rock wall.

Suta climbed up on her mother's back, just like the monkeys she had watched so often. She clung to Mia, with her feet planted firmly on her mother's hips and her arms gripping her shoulders. This gave Mia the freedom to climb without restriction, but the dark night and hard rain all but blinded her. She was forced to wait for lightning flashes to fully comprehend the severity of her dilemma.

The top edge of the wall loomed high above them, but once the danger of being swept away was over, slow and careful action was needed or they would still surely perish. It might well take the rest of the night, but Mia was determined get herself and her daughter to safety. *Just make every movement count, and always look all around you before going forward,* Mia could hear her mother say when she was teaching her to be independent. She would soon teach Suta everything she knew about how to survive in the world, but the child had already learned so much. Mia marveled at how Suta could already feed herself, seeking out and finding herbs and mushrooms on her own.

By the time mother and daughter reached the ledge, dawn was painting the eastern sky with swirls of light-gray clouds. The storm had ended, but the day promised to be wet, and a chilled breeze was picking up from the north. Mia's body screamed for relief, and her neck ached from looking up for hours.

When she finally pulled herself and Suta onto what was a grassy flatland, the two lay motionless for some time, scanning the wide expanse for anything that moved. Surprising a hungry predator at first light would not be wise, and Mia looked around for someplace safe where they could hide and rest without being discovered.

Testing the air for scents that presaged danger, but smelling nothing untoward, Mia sat up and peered over the edge of the cliff they had just scaled. Her village had been washed away in its entirety. Her Heart became heavy with the thought of losing her friends and family and the very real possibility of never again seeing Suta's father, Rugas. He was much older than Mia, but this didn't matter to her. He was kind and funny. He had been gone for two moons with a hunting party, so he was not in the village at the time of the storm. There was no way of knowing where he was now, what kind of damage had occurred elsewhere, or if he would ever return.

Mia fought back the hot tears that pressed against her cheeks. She didn't want Suta to see that she was upset. Survival meant control at all times. She and her daughter had no choice but to now assume they would be nomads unless fate somehow reunited them with their people. But the chance of this happening was slim. Her people were the only Valley Dwellers that she knew about from the old stories. Other people, different from her, lived in caves or on the Flats. She had seen the Cave Dwellers before from a distance, but never those people known as Flats. She was staring at a huge, grassy plain and wondering if many Flats lived there, but more important, if they would welcome or instead want to kill her and her daughter. The tales she'd heard had depicted Flats as equally intolerable and violent.

Mia could make out a herd of mammoths off in the distance, which at first looked like a slow-moving black stain drifting across the green prairie. She wondered absently if maybe Rugas and the other hunters in his party were stalking them. Mammoths were not an easy kill, but Rugas was an excellent hunter. The hunting parties traveled far and were gone for long stretches of time, so Rugas wouldn't know yet about the village disaster. It would be wonderful if their paths crossed and they could all be reunited somehow. Yet what were the chances? Certainly not good.

The rain started up again, this time the drops hitting her as sharply as if they were frozen needles, reminding her that the snow season would soon arrive. Suta was cold and shivering, and Mia's stomach was growling for food. They had to find shelter and set a snare, and Mia was exhausted.

The two set out, walking the edge of the cliff and hoping to come upon a cave or rock outcropping that would serve as protection from the rain and wind. It wasn't long before they followed the ground as it sloped into a canyon and widened into a natural pathway. Mia was relieved to find many trees and thick clumps of bushes, the underbrush assuring the presence of small game that would be easy to catch in a snare or drop with a well-aimed stone or spear. But this meant that large predators, such as wolves and lions, would be close by as well. So Mia's first order of business was to fashion a sturdy, sharp spear, not only for food but for protection.

The mother and daughter passed a couple of shallow caves before discovering one that would house them comfortably and provide safety.

They had to climb to reach it, and it had a flat, clear opening perfect for building a fire. Mia signaled for Suta to wait while she carefully checked out everything inside. It was quiet and safe and dry, so they went about the business of gathering twigs and limbs, and they constructed a rock pit for cooking.

Mia felt for the leather pouch that always hung around her waist. As a preparation for emergencies, everyone from the village carried a pouch similar to Mia's. She emptied its contents onto the cave's floor. There was a flint for fire, a very sharp skinning tool, a digging tool, a spool of strong twine, and several stones. A light piece of woven cloth would serve as a covering to put over bedding. Healing herbs and some hard, smoked meat were wrapped in a smaller pouch made of animal hide.

Mia took Suta with her to explore the immediate area. In a clearing, she showed her young daughter how to construct a snare and cover it with loose brush in hope of catching a rabbit or squirrel. With that done, they collected and piled leaves and ferns for bedding. After starting a small but crackling fire at the mouth of the cave, they shared a meal of dried meat Mia fortunately had stored in her pouch, and together they fell into a deep sleep.

The rain had stopped sometime during the night, and the bright orb of the moon bathed the land in soft light. Mia went out to check the snare, and to her delight she found it had secured a large rabbit. She killed it and tied the carcass to her belt and reset the snare. Farther down the path, the river ran high and close to the shore. Some fish had been tossed to the bank and stranded there. Mia strung them next to the rabbit. Then she sat and watched the churning waters, wondering how all this had happened. Her people had lived in that valley for as long as she could remember, with never a threat of flooding, everyone unprepared for the disaster that came in the night.

Many of her people had been swept away in their sleep, particularly the elders. Her mother, grandmother, grandfather, and two cousins all lived together. Her mother would have lingered to help everyone else in her family escape, but there was so little time. Mia herself had just made the cliff wall, and by sheer luck. If Suta had been with her in bed and not outside the hut, maybe Mia could have helped save her family, but such thoughts were empty. For now, Mia had wandered too far and for too long from the cave—and Suta. Instinct pulled at her to hurry back, so she ran as fast as her legs would carry her.

Approaching the cave, she spotted a pair of four-legged shapes lurking in the shadows. The fire was just a glow, so she couldn't see well, and she blamed herself for not adding more brush before she left to check the snare. With Suta her primary concern, Mia's whole body was primed for whatever awaited her.

She ran toward the lurking shapes, uttering a guttural scream and flailing her arms. Too small for wolves but too big for foxes, they were likely wolf dogs. The element of surprise worked, and the two predators jumped away. Picking up several large stones, she threw them as hard as she could, hearing a distinct yip and a louder howl signaling she'd hit her marks.

Mia arrived to find Suta at the rear of the cave, armed with her own stones, in an attack pose. Mia was impressed with her youngster's courage and for remembering her Life lessons. Mia ran to Suta's side and hugged her daughter. The animals were gone, at least for now. But when the food was cooking, they would be back with more of their pack. No matter, Mia and Suta would be ready for them.

The rabbit roasted over the fire while the fish fried on a flat, hot rock. The meal was enormously satisfying, and mother and daughter talked about their destroyed village and what they would do next. Suta was a smart child, a survivor. She could understand many things Mia was telling her, and the little girl, who would be four by the next full moon, would instinctively react if danger presented itself. This calmed Mia somewhat.

The wolf dogs soon returned, as Mia had predicted, but they howled a few times and hung beyond the bushes and rocks, on the path below the cave, doing nothing more. She found it odd that there were just two of them. Perhaps they were outcasts, or a breed that traveled in pairs. It would soon be dawn, and they would surely be gone at first light. But Mia would be wrong. She and Suta discovered them lying on the lower path when they went to forage for mushrooms or fruit for their next meal.

They were not like wolf dogs Mia had seen before. These animals had dense smooth coats and long sloping heads. Their bodies were strong and muscular, and they didn't skulk around like wolves but sat quietly upright, taking in everything with obviously keen eyesight.

Mia had seen sand paintings of these types of animals when she was a child and her village had visited another clan. She remembered images on rock walls, drawings depicting the Flats people with these animals hunting in pairs, running alongside their prey, unlike wolves who stalked in a pack and overwhelmed their quarry with sheer numbers.

These wolf dogs would run their prey until it dropped from exhaustion. However, the Flats people would take the dead animals from them because these dogs had a timid personality when it came to man. Mia had thought that their behavior was perhaps a token of respect, as the cat will bow to the bear. Yes, respect was a good word for these dogs. They seemed content to stay near both Mia and Suta, interested in what they were doing but not acting in any way aggressive.

Still, Mia supposed that these wolf dogs preferred attacking in open spaces. And she and Suta had now arrived at the edge of the Flats! Keeping her distance, and a spear she'd fashioned at her side, Mia studied the dogs as she and Suta searched out tubers and herbs.

Later that evening, while eating tubers and what remained of the rabbit caught in the snare, Mia noticed one dog sidling closer to the cave's mouth. It eyed the meat she was eating, and a long tendril of drool hung from the corner of its mouth. Mia looked at the meat and thought twice about what would happen if . . . if she extended her hand with the food in it toward the wild dog. Fear was something good to have because it heightened one's awareness of the surroundings. This, however, was an entirely different kind of fear she was experiencing.

Very cautiously, with its eyes riveted on Mia, the dog crawled slowly toward her, and it gently took the gift in its mouth. The dog's eyes and Mia's locked for just a moment, but long enough that she felt an unfamiliar tugging at her Heart. A bridge had been crossed somewhere in both their lives. The connection was made, and from out of nowhere Mia felt a pang of love for the wolf dog. She cried.

Mia looked over at Suta, the child nodding off and breathing softly, sated after her meal. Mia dearly missed her family, and she was unsure how she and Suta would manage to survive alone—and for how long. Mia hugged her knees and cried again.

3

"This Hu-man is sad and unsure of herself," I said to my sister, Seeba, who was pulling hard with her teeth at a thistle embedded in her paw.

"So what?" Seeba replied as she chewed on the pad of her paw and then pushed the thorn off her tongue. "Come on, let's run away from this place. We have hunting to do on the prairie and mates to find; little ones to raise. Why you are staying here with these Hu-mans, I don't know. We're here to balance The Earth Mother. Hu-mans have their own Plan to follow."

I turned to face her. She was the largest of the siblings from our litter, and a fine hunting companion. She was also my best friend on the other side of the Bridge. It was fun coming to live on The Earth Mother in the same reincarnation time with her.

"I don't know, Seeba." I said, vigorously scratching my ear. "I think this might be *my* Hu-man."

Seeba got to her feet and circled around me until she faced me again. "Puck, nothing was said about a Hu-man on this journey. We're here to serve The Earth Mother. We're supposed to balance the Life here: Life and death. That's all I remember. Azul said nothing to me about a

Hu-man. You'd be overstepping the Plan for us if you were to stay here with this Hu-man."

"I think I need to stay, sis. I just have this . . . this feeling."

Seeba jumped at me, baring her teeth. "Fine! Stay and be the fool when your hide is draped around their shoulders and your meat is in their stomachs."

I bared my teeth at her, but in jest. "Well, then, isn't that a Balance in itself? There are many of us who do just that, sacrificing our bodies as well as our lives for others to survive and complete their missions here. I feel something I've never felt before. If I'm wrong, Azul will tell me somehow. I'm staying." I whined gently. "But you can go if you must."

"Good luck, foolish one," she said over her shoulder as she trotted toward the brush. "If this is not your mission, I'll see you at some point with the Flats." She stopped and turned to me, lowering her head and licking her lips as a sign of pack love and acceptance, adding softly, "Be careful, Puck." I never saw my sister again throughout this stay on The Earth Mother.

━ ⌒

Mia and the little Hu-man wandered for many days, and I could tell they were getting tired and desperate to find more of their pack. I would have helped them, but I couldn't detect a scent anywhere that hinted of more Hu-mans nearby.

I don't know why, but I was drawn toward the older Hu-man. She shared her meals with me and never chased me away. Once, I brought a fresh kill and left it by her while she slept. This female looked at me strangely after that, but not in a bad way. It felt almost natural for me to bring her and the other Hu-man food, as my mother had brought food for me.

Many times, as we walked together, I would flush out game for her to kill with her stones. It made me feel good to be of some service. On stormy nights, I could sense her relax inside the shelter they used, knowing I was outside with an ear for approaching danger. I sensed that I made her feel safe. But we still kept our distance. We had an uneasy companionship, one built out of respect for our intended ways.

The Earth Mother had been warning us that she'd already turned her back on the sun, and the weather did indeed turn frigid quite suddenly. I could see that Mia was growing even more anxious as winter set in. I, myself, was uncomfortable in the often cold, needlelike rain, as my coat wasn't as full and thick as cousin wolf's. Dog of this species were the real lovers of the cold. My kind, however, usually roamed farther to the south, where the breezes, while stiff in winter, don't wield the bite they deliver here.

My sister probably found others of our kind and had already moved on. I missed her, and I would be telling a falsehood if I said I wasn't concerned for my prospects for surviving a true winter. I howled at night in the quiet moonlight in hope of a reply from Dog, but any of my species were too far away.

I desperately wanted to be with Dog, but I stayed with my new pack members; these two furless creatures who hunted poorly by my standards and needed to make the burning light to warm themselves to keep all animals away. I, for one, would never consider coming close to the burning light that consumed all. I saw it once come from the sky and take away a whole forest and its creatures, leaving the land barren afterwards.

I knew my place with these Hu-mans, and it was always to keep a safe distance from them. Yes, close enough to sense and feel their needs, but far enough away to remain free and roam as I pleased.

I never saw nor sensed the big cat, which was very unusual for me. It happened at night as we all slept. From my resting place, not far away from the cave's mouth, I heard Mia's screams and sprang up, confused. Hearing her scream again, I bolted to the cave's entrance just as the big cat was dragging Suta away. It's the way of the cat to quickly break the neck of its prey with its powerful jaws, and the little Hu-man was limp in its mouth.

I lunged at the cat and tore into the large feline, peeling off a sizable flap of skin from a hind quarter as it raced from the cave. But, as with any cat, it would not drop its prize. I sped after it, hoping for another chance. To my dismay, as if a ghost, it vanished into deep woods. I stopped my chase. The shifty creature had run farther and faster than I could keep up. Suta was gone!

I ran back to the cave and was met by Mia's scream. Her fingernails were ripped off from her clawing the ground. Her groans and screams continued all that night and into the next, her loud anguish quieted only when her tears overcame her. I sat quietly and watched her odd Human behavior until long after dark that second night. I understood that she knew Suta was dead when the cat took her from the cave. I also recognized a brutal emptiness that hung everywhere. What I found puzzling was her attachment to this feeling of loss. For Dog, and many animals like us, we accept death as a way back to our Home at the Bridge. Death isn't a loss, it's our way of going back Home, where there's rest and the fullness of a Summerland, and, of course, the soft, awakening, loving touch provided by Azul.

I sighed and thought of Azul, wondering if Hu-mans had the same wonderful place to go as we did at the end of our experience Here. I also thought of Mia, now alone with no other Hu-man. I was hungry, and she'd had nothing to eat either. She had not created her warming light for all this time, and the temperate was now freezing cold. On this night, a bitter wind blew ice mixed with snow, and everything rushed around in a frenzy.

I watched Mia lay her body down against the frigid wind and roll over on her side. I could sense how cold she was, how hunger was robbing her strength, how she longed to be with Suta, wherever that might be. I could sense her letting go of Life, just as other animals do when they wander off to die, or in Dog way before we travel back to our real Home.

I lay down and put my head between my paws and watched her from afar, when I heard the angelic voice of Azul: "Puck, your Hu-man needs you now. Go to her. Your new journey has begun. Remember, you are The Love of The Most High. Be Dog!"

So, I did what my angel told me to do. I walked over to Mia and curled my body tightly against hers. I allowed my breath to warm her and my fur to shelter her from the elements. And at that moment I claimed this Hu-man for my own.

4

Exhausted from her profound grief, Mia slept until well after the sun came up. When she awoke, she felt around with her hands but didn't move otherwise. I heard her breath shorten into fearful little pants. I lifted my head, which rested at her shoulder, and looked into her eyes. We were so close that I felt a twinge of dangerous excitement that comes with stepping into the unknown. However, instead of rolling away in fear and grabbing a stick to attack me, she closed her eyes and offered her throat, wanting to die and asking me to take her.

Prey often did this when confronted with no way out. The defeated animal turned and faced its enemy, or slowed its pace so it could be run down easily. For an instant, my wild nature teased me. Killing her would be easy. I could smell her submissiveness, and I was beyond hungry. Mia was now food, and I could sink my teeth into her throat and she would be gone. Her meat would sustain me for a week, at least, and I could find Seeba and my pack and live like Dog.

I drew back my lips and growled, calling her out: "Do you want this? I come with Life or with death. Whatever you desire, you choose." If Human was as wild as all Life Here, she would understand what I said to her. But did she hear me? Would she bolt and give me a reason to tear her to pieces? Would she say something back to me? I was listening, but . . .

She stretched her neck, making herself even more vulnerable to my jaws. I could taste her warm blood. She grabbed a fistful of my fur in anticipation of her impending death. My growl grew into a snarl and I began to salivate. I was about to clamp down on her neck when she turned her head and gazed into my eyes. I closed my mouth and whined as I heard Azul.

"Puck, you are being offered a new Plan, but of course you may choose your own way. Still, you know who you are and what is expected of you now. Many animals balance The Earth Mother; few are called to teach Hu-mans about Love, Respect and Honor. This is the path you are ready to follow, if you so choose. Yours is the gift to teach and be taught the ways of All That Is, which is The Way of Francis. Only those animals that have gained this awareness thus far are presented with this opportunity. Do what you will. Any decision you make will be honored. You may open the door with your jaws for Mia to continue her journey in Spirit, or you may grow with her through many Lifetimes to reach perfect Love. She is your Hu-man now, either way."

I softened my resolve and rested my head across Mia's sacrificial neck. It took a moment, but she slowly released her hold on my fur and opened her fingers and stroked my coat. Her breathing returning to normal, and she watched me with caution as I sat up and pricked my ears toward the front of the cave. I wagged my tail and allowed my face to convey this message: "Come on, get up! There's a rabbit waiting to jump into our stomachs!"

Mia stood on shaky feet and stared at me for what seemed like the longest time. I swept my tail across the dirt floor, sending dry leaves scattering, which caused her to smile slightly. She extended her hand to me and I licked it, tasting the salt of who she was. She touched the top of my head and then picked up her hunting stones. She'd heard me! I felt like a puppy again. I leaped around in crazy circles and bounced ahead of her down the path. Although her profound sadness at losing Suta was evident by new lines on her face, I sensed her gaining strength and a definite desire to keep living. We were off on the first venture of living many lives together.

Mia might have known my purpose, but I don't think so. After all, I *am* Dog. I'm the teacher. I'm the vessel that holds the Love. I'm the mirror of Forgiveness. That's why my name spelled backwards is God. I remembered in perfect clarity The Prayer of Francis. I had taught my first lesson—and it was Trust.

— —

We spent the winter months enjoying each other, teaching and learning so many things by way of our new mutual communication. I showed her different stalking techniques and the need for patience, which she had little tolerance for. She, in turn, taught me her language and certain hand signals to obey: "stay," "come," "sit," and, with prey, "kill."

I gave her my name, and I was delighted when she put a sound to it: Puck. She understood me as well as I understood her, her commands mostly without sounds but sometimes through whistles and calls. For her part, she recognized the meanings of my barks, my whines, my expressions. We played together and wondered about each other. These months were very good, both of us very happy and content with Life, enjoying the companionship we craved.

Every night we told each other our personal stories as we rested in the cave, protected from the howling winter storms, our faces painted with the flames of the warming light I had now come to appreciate. Had it not been for Suta's untimely death, I questioned if our friendship would have progressed this far. I often thought about The Plan that all living things have on The Earth Mother, my Plan to oversee Mia but learn the lessons of Life Here from her, and my Plan to teach the lessons of The Most High to her. Azul was always reminding us at Home on The **Bridge, "All things are connected. Trust *your* Plan." But did my Hu-man have the same Plan?

— —

Early spring was a time when The Earth Mother instilled energy into her children and caused all of us to wander and seek out new lives. Spring not only blessed our bodies with warm sunshine, but it provided a healing effect from the harshness of winter that stirred our Souls as well. It was a time for exploring, finding food sources, and mating with others of our species. Hu-man and Dog seemed the same in these regards.

Mia grew restless, wanting to find her pack and taking me farther on our journeys. As much as I adored Mia's company, I found myself torn between staying or going, often howling my loneliness into the black nights in hope of an answer, from my pack, riding back on the wind. I missed my species as much as my Hu-man missed hers.

One spring day, as we picked our way down a rocky plateau, I spotted a pack of Dog roaming in the distance. My Heart raced with excitement, and I couldn't restrain myself from running around Mia, telling her of my discovery. She ruffled my fur playfully and gave me the signal to go. She was now so good at knowing me. I ran a short distance, turned and begged her to come, too, but she was busy preparing a campsite and stayed.

It required considerable time before these strange Dog accepted me. I suspected that the Hu-man scent which lingered on me was foreign to them, along with the fact that they weren't my breed. These Dog had dense coats and heavy bodies. They couldn't run as fast as I could, but they had enough brute strength to take down a bear or bull mammoth if they teamed up. They were an odd pack, content to lie around and pant, lapping up long strands of saliva, which hung like icicles from the sides of their wide mouths. They had come down from the mountains to find prey, but their home Here was a place of cold and snow, and they would be returning to it.

I thought of Mia often, and when I'd finally overstayed my welcome with this cordial group of Dog, I wandered back to where I'd left her. But her camp was empty! The warming light had gone out, and it appeared to me that it had been days since it even flickered. There was a strange sensation in the air around the camp that gave me concern. Adding to my worry, Mia's leather bag was gone but certain items from it remained. I turned them over with my nose, searching for clues to what had happened. An unpleasant, sour smell suddenly hurt my nostrils, and I felt queasy. What was it I sensing? What was that scent? The odor must belong to a Hu-man with a dark, dangerous nature, and he'd been here in Mia's camp.

I wasn't familiar with many Hu-man scents, but I remembered, when very young in this Life, coming across a band of Hu-man hunters. Each Hu-man had its own special scent, as with all living animals, with no two ever alike. Some smells were light and clean; Mia's was sweet, as was Suta's. But some were dark and heavy, like this one that now filled my head. However, there was another scent as well—Mia's fear. I bounded off on a trail that I hoped would lead me to my beloved Hu-man.

For three days I trotted tirelessly, seeking Mia. The trail was simple to follow, as every day the scent became stronger. It also became clear that this evil Hu-man was as one with her.

I soon came across a barrage of different scents. The pack of Humans was nearby. My Mia was close—as well as that horrible, pungent smell of danger that identified with *him*. Every part of me bristled, ready for a fight. I slunk my way to the edge of a precipice, where, not far below me, a camp was set up. The smell of freshly cooked meat and newly cut hides filled the air.

This Hu-man pack was a large one. I saw their noisy pups they called children running around with adult Hu-mans who tried to control them. Many warming lights flickered on paths that led to strange, round shelters. A few canines had picked up on my scent and barked a warning for me to stay where I was, but I inched closer. Soon, however, I lay down and waited for them to get bored before I would move again.

Under the cover of darkness, I made my way to the edge of the camp. I surprised one of the dogs, who sprang up and barked furiously. But when I struck a submissive pose and licked my lips as a sign of friendship, as well as lowering my head and wagging my tail, he welcomed me. I guessed that he smelled Mia's scent on me, even though we had been parted many weeks, and this was really why his aggression changed and he continued to posture a pleasant greeting.

We sat and shared our feelings for a while as the other dogs came by and cautiously accepted me. They told me their role in camp was to alert the Hu-mans of danger. They warned me, if a Hu-man saw me with them, they would have no choice but to attack. They also told me that the Hu-man female I sought was tied up, like a captured animal, in a hut at the back of the camp.

I crept on my belly to the rear of the camp to see for myself. It was true. Mia lay on a patch of dirt, her hands and feet bound by a rawhide strap. The skins she wore for clothes were torn, and I didn't need to be Dog to sense her pain and anguish, as she was hungry, weak, and bleeding. The heavy, awful smell of the evil Hu-man male lingered everywhere. I crawled close enough for her to sense me, but she did not. Something was very wrong. Mia was not aware of anything but her misery. I backed away and watched from afar, trying to figure out what it all meant. I needed to understand what was happening in her world—and in mine.

When no Hu-man was looking, I stole a hunk of meat from a warming pit and ran up to the edge of the woods to eat it. Before long I observed the evil Hu-man male walking around the camp. I was told by one of the dogs that he was called Hazz. He was cruel and beat the dogs and killed living things when he felt like it. The other Hu-mans, in this "village" as they referred to it, had wanted to banish this Hu-man because of his horrible ways. But no one dared challenge him.

Crin, a female who had taken a liking to me, told me, "Hazz is the worst of his Hu-man kind. He is like a terrible alpha dog." I nodded my understanding of the example she'd used as she continued, "He has no respect for The Earth Mother. He's often angry for no reason. The people of the village think he's mad."

Crin shared that all Dog in her pack were stolen from their den, before their eyes had even opened, so living with these Hu-mans was normal for them, even though they knew of their Divine Dog natures.

The Dog in this pack listened in awe as I spoke of Azul and my new role as teacher for this female Hu-man, Mia. I told them of my choice to serve her from now on and not The Earth Mother.

"We are still serving The Earth Mother," Crin's brother, Dob, said. "We come to help balance Hu-man presence Here, as we, too, have been placed Here with a different Plan from our wild sisters and brothers. In fact, our mission is also teaching Hu-mans, but you, Puck . . . you are obviously the chosen one. We honor you." All Dog whined their soft approval, as I was now encircled by this pack.

"I'm not sure what to do now," I said and growled my concern. "Do I stay close to Mia, or do I just find my pack and forget all this? I'm not sure what's expected of me, and Azul is silent. I've no Plan except that I need to free Mia somehow."

"Well, it would seem to me, that *is* the Plan," another of Crin's siblings, Gotoh, said. "I am the eldest, therefore the wisest. And I say, how can you teach someone who is held captive by another? So free this Human, Mia, and go away with her. The Plan you came to Earth with is the right one, even though you're not sure what it is or how it's supposed to develop. You must rely on Faith and Faith alone. If you make the wrong decision, you will know soon enough to take corrective action."

The entire pack began sauntering back to camp, but Gotoh stopped and turned to me. "Wait for our signal, then go free your Mia. And good luck. Perhaps we'll meet one day at The Bridge."

Dob, who was the last to depart, said softly as he passed me, "I wish I were good enough to be assigned a Hu-man to teach. I wish I could be that smart, that good-hearted, that Divine—"

I rubbed my nose against him. "Dob, you are Divine. As are all Dog in your pack. We all possess the Love of All That Is. We are Dog, never forget that. Just wait for your Plan. It will surely come, for we're all on the same path leading into The Heart of Love. Every one of us will, in time, show a Hu-man the way to The Most High. Just always remember to abide by the Rules of Francis."

5

Gotoh did not disappoint. The pack summoned a Wolf cousin to help them create a diversion. The plan was for the pack to furiously chase this lone Wolf through the camp and run around Hazz's den, which would flush out this awful Hu-man. Then I was to go free Mia.

I lay outside, where I could see Mia crouched at the back of Hazz's animal-hide-covered den. I studied the straps that bound her. I should be able to gnaw through them, but having adequate time was crucial. Would I have enough?

Everything occurred like a sudden storm. The pack yelped and tore through the camp, amid the screams of the Hu-man pack members. All Dog ran around in a frenzy, snapping at the tail of Wolf, who dashed into Hazz's den where Mia was being held captive.

I had to act quickly, so I ran to Mia, who awoke with a start and screamed. When she saw me, she turned her hands toward me. I tore ferociously at her binding, but the strap didn't break. I did, however, manage to pull her feet free, and we ran from the camp. I could hear the dogs off in the distance, pretending to track Wolf. The question was, how long would the ploy work?

Mia was weak and could hardly keep up with me, soon sinking to her knees and sobbing. It was apparent she was spent. I tried my best to raise her, but Hazz had spotted us and was running our way, swinging a club. This meant death for me, so I had no choice but to retreat. I would be of no use to Mia if injured—or worse.

Hazz dragged Mia back to his den, and the camp was once again quiet. My Heart wasn't quiet, though. It was filled with hatred, all focused on the name of Hazz. Fortunately for me and Wolf, the pack wasn't sent to look for either of us.

I paced all night, growling to myself, consumed with this feeling of hatred. The scent of this horrible Hu-man remained with me. It signified the existence of someone very disturbed. As wild Dog, I had never experienced anything as intense as what I was feeling now, exceeding even the anxiety surrounding the Life-or-death challenge that often arose between alpha males. My current obsession was different.

I wanted Hazz's blood. I wanted his Life to cease. It was not a matter of banishing an infringing male of my species from the pack. I wanted Hazz's Life. I wanted him forever dead. I wanted to kill him for what he had done to Mia. So right before dawn I went to Hazz's den. He was sleeping. Mia lifted up when she saw me. I could sense both her relief and her concern. And something else—happiness.

I wagged my tail at the sight of her and turned my attention to Hazz. I curled my lips back to expose my fangs and uttered a low growl. Hazz was quickly on his feet, but surprised and unprepared. I lunged at his throat, missing, but tore the flesh on his shoulder. He screamed, and the commotion brought the pack in a howling run our way, but instead of attacking me they scurried around us, barking. So, again and again, I ripped into this putrid-smelling human, my teeth shredding muscle and tendons and causing him great pain. I hated him with every fiber of my body, and when I finally did sever an artery, I yelped in glee as he fell and bled out. I heard the other dogs rejoicing as well. I'd performed a good and heroic deed. I had killed Hazz.

The melee had taken us outside the hut, with Hazz lying in a pile of bloody dirt at the entrance. Many Hu-mans circled around us. They saw Hazz was dead, so they turned their attention to me. They would not be wrong in their assessment that I might be a canine with the "mad" disease. With fresh blood in my mouth, and my wildness peaked to survival mode, I was ready to fight whoever and whatever now came my way.

The Hu-mans held sticks with warming fires on the ends and taunted me with their spears. I snarled and glowered at each one, and dared any sort of movement that would give me reason to shred the entire lot of these Hu-mans, if I could. I was indeed "mad." I heard Dob say to Gotoh, "These Hu-mans are assembled as one. They will kill him now. It's too bad he's not a Dog of the mountain type, for as fierce as he is he could take them all."

Now that I knew Mia was safe from Hazz, my impending doom meant little to me. I felt the various pricks and jabs from their fire sticks and spears as they tried to get me into position for the kill.

Mia appeared from the hut, her hands held high in the universal language for halting whatever was happening. I watched her enter the pack of Hu-mans, who uttered mutterings of surprise. She stooped and opened her arms to me, and I respectfully went to her. I was still taken by rage, but she quelled my fire with the gentle rain of her touch. I melted into her.

The Hu-mans quieted, but their astonishment lasted for only a few moments before chaos began anew. Some Hu-mans knelt before Mia, asking her Blessings. as surely she must be a Chosen One possessing unfathomable wisdom. Other Hu-mans, however, backed away in terror, calling Mia an enchantress, a black force that would bring evil to the camp.

The women of this pack of Hu-mans, having great power, as all primitive adult females possessed in any camp, came forward and lifted Mia to her feet. They had witnessed this coming together of nurturing woman and savage beast, and Mia was declared a Sacred Being of The Feminine Earth. They draped her in holy robes and demanded that all Hu-mans in the camp bow to her in acceptance of this miraculous event.

I followed after Mia as the Hu-man women eyed me with caution and wonder, only to gasp in shock when a spear entered my side. Mia dropped to her knees and cradled my head, weeping and stroking my fur. The women vilified the offending male Hu-man, who claimed he had the approval of those in his pack who perceived Mia as a threat and therefore me as well. A great discussion ensued concerning the degrading of so mystical an omen as Mia and the righteousness of killing me.

The camp settled into an uneasy alliance. That night I passed into Spirit easily, as I was in the loving arms of my beloved Mia. I trusted the power of the Hu-man females to keep her safe, and I accepted the sad reality that what Hu-mans don't understand, they fear; and, what they fear, they kill.

— —

I'm awake when I arrive at The Bridge, and the awe of being Home takes my breath away. I sit in the soft grass and collect my thoughts. Usually, Dog arrives Home to The Summerland in a gentle way, full of the loving anticipation of the welcoming arms of our angel guide. I look for Azul but don't see her right off. Soon, however, I catch sight of her walking toward me. I jump up and run to her, but her expression stops me cold. Still, I press her to see me.

"Azul! I'm back!" I yelp at her, expecting a broad smile, but she has no warmth to show me today. Instead, her beautiful face is stern. I know I'm in trouble, yet I keep at it, "Did you see what I did, Azul? I protected my Mia from a terrible man! I killed him, and now he will never harm another living Soul. I did a good deed!"

Azul's voice is soft yet deeply grave. "You did not do a good deed, Puck. You took a Life in anger. You gave in to the emotion of hatred— and acted upon it. You killed a man who was doing nothing more than sleeping."

"No, no Azul!" I bark. "Hazz was a demon! He was a cruel man who killed for enjoyment. He held Mia captive, and she was suffering horribly in his grip. Both camp packs cheered when he died, both Hu-man and Dog. Mia is now free because of me. How is that not a good deed?"

Aluz gives me grim look. "You interfered with another's Plan. Dog never acts out of hatred. You have broken one of the major laws handed down by All That Is. You did not kill because of protection or self-defense, you killed from a dark place; a place borne of your personal judgment."

"I'm confused," I say, not exaggerating in the least. "I saved Mia. Isn't that what I'm supposed to do? Serve and protect her at all costs?"

"This would be so if your lives were being threatened. But that wasn't the case. You committed premeditated murder. That was a very unwise act, to put it mildly. Now you will have this burden following you throughout your Life until you find a way to right it."

"I don't know why this is so terrible!" I bark at her in defiance. "I don't understand this lesson at all!" Azul takes me in her arms and I cry against her breast. "I'm so sorry Azul, but I don't understand . . . I—"

She rubs my nose. "Every being has a Plan set before birth; the higher Souls, the teaching Souls and the Souls that are struggling to learn. There are no good or bad Souls. Hu-mans are all fighting some kind of battle in their lives on earth, trying to balance the Light and the Dark and trying to find the good path Home. How do you know that man's Heart would not have changed for the better at some time in his Life?" Her eyes pierce mine and give me shivers. "It was not for you to judge him. A Hu-man's Heart can change instantly when touched by pure Love. He always had a choice between good and evil. You took that choice away in this Lifetime. And he will always remember that you did. Now, you have made an enemy. Your Path will be noticeably harder now. Not only must you teach Mia throughout her Lifetimes to give and accept unconditional Love, you must find some way to remedy the wrong you've done to Hazz. Do you hear what I'm saying? This is a profound lesson, Puck."

I shoot her what I have to guess is a stupid look. I never thought it possible to feel this miserable at The Bridge, but I'm now filled with profound regret. "Will I be going back to Mia soon?" I ask, already knowing what the answer will be.

"No, Puck, not for a while," Azul says, validating my fear and adding, "You have some serious thinking to do first."

The mood at The Bridge is jovial and carefree for the most part. It's like recess at school. The lessons are still in your mind, but for the time being they're lost in play; that is, until you're called back in to class. Yet sometimes even play cannot hide the ever-looming presence of making a bad decision. I disappointed Azul as well as myself.

I'm sitting on a grassy overlook, looking at all the peaceful animals grazing and basking in the heavenly sunlight, but my thoughts are far away. I'm trying desperately to sort out my past-Life's transgressions when a voice I know says, "I heard you were back. I expected to see you at your welcome-home party, but here you are instead."

"Seeba!" I jump up with joy at the sight of best friend and sister in my past Life. "What are you doing here?"

Seeba lies down next to me and sighs. "Old age brought me Home. I starved on the Flats one winter, and I grew feeble. It wasn't so bad, though. I just went to sleep in the snow and woke up here." She laughs. "What about you, my brother? How are you doing?"

"Oh, dear Seeba, I don't know where to begin . . . I just—"

"You don't have to say anything more. I know all about what happened to you and Mia."

This news makes my ears perk up. "You do? How do you know? Did you see my Mia? Is she still on Earth? What's happened since my death?"

Seeba laughs. "One question at a time, my brother. I was very near the camp when you tried to rescue Mia, but of course I didn't know it then. I met an old Dog from the pack who'd wandered off to die on the Flats. She was sick and wanted to go Home, so she left the others and I saw her bed down beside the trail I was following. I remember her name was Crin. She told me this amazing story about how you, a few Earth years earlier, had killed a very evil man who'd taken Mia for his slave wife. You are a legend among Dog everywhere on Earth, since not only did you fight bravely but remained oddly loyal to the female Hu-man, Mia. Yes, this relationship created much curiosity. You were highly renowned on Earth, but Mia was even more revered."

"Mia! Tell me about Mia. Is she still there? Is she well?"

"Crin told me that she had passed into Spirit, but before she left Earth she'd stayed at that camp because she was worshiped as a holy woman called a Shaman. Everyone looked up to her as if she possessed some sort of magic that enabled her to communicate with animals. I suspect you had something to do with this, dear brother, as close as you were to her. Crin said she'd witnessed Mia healing another canine. Afterwards, all the Hu-mans wanted her to heal them as well. They considered her touched by the gods because of the way she was brought to them—in the hands of a madman—and because of her gentle, wise ways of communicating with The Earth Mother."

"Oh, my, Seeba, I'm so relieved to learn that she was safe all those years. But . . . the *gods*?" What does that mean?"

Seeba laughs again and rolls over, letting the Heavenly sun warm her belly. "Hu-mans are such a funny bunch, and very backward in their thinking. They have all sorts of stone images they pray to and honor. How unenlightened must one be, not to see All That Is? And that All That Is remains alive in everything and everyone? Hu-mans don't understand this. They believe that God, as they call it, is separate from them and their lives. So they make images they can see, statues and symbols they can talk to, and they follow other Hu-mans they believe know something more than they do. They ask for protection, food, healing— when all they have to do is exist. We know that all our needs and desires will be met without question or hesitation. We believe in The Plan set out for each and every one of us, as Dog is never denied the Love and care of The Most High, but Hu-mans sadly think they have to be worthy to accept what their God gives to them."

"If this is so, in my next Life with Mia, how am I going to teach her about Divine Love?"

"I think she already understands full well. According to Crin, Mia was teaching Hu-mans about the natural Trust of the Universe to provide for them. From what Crin said, half of the camp followed Mia and the other half was against her." Seeba rose on her haunches. "Now you know all I know. I left and joined up with my pack and lived for quite a while longer, doing what we wild Dog do before I came Home." Seeba pants happily before adding, "I had many puppies, all well and fat, who became honored pack members. I had a very good Life on Earth this time."

I lap my sister's face. "I'm glad for you, Seeba, and grateful for the news you've brought me. It's so good to see you." I back away and whine, and Seeba is quick to catch my mood.

"Why are you unhappy when at Home, of all places?"

I tell Seeba about my meeting with Azul and how confused I am as to how I am to correct my wrongdoing.

"Puck, learn from your own teachings of Trust. Be patient. You don't have to do anything now. Trust and wait on the will of All That Is to show you the perfect Path to the most perfect way." Seeba gets up to leave, but she rubs against me as a farewell gesture. "And don't forget, my dear brother, to Love yourself in the process. Love is everything that's good about Dog."

After my talk with Seeba, I spend a lot of time by myself thinking. Finally, I guess enough is enough, because Azul finds me and says the timing is right for me to join up with Mia again. What a wonderful surprise! She says, with a wide smile covering her beautiful face, to just go and be Dog and to pay attention to what Life has to offer; the good as well as the bad. She hints that this Lifetime will be a better one in order that I might regain the Trust I lost through my mistake with Hazz. She leaves me with, "Go and look into the mirror, Puck, and see that which you are looking at is looking back at you."

6

I was born within a little nest of white bunny fur and feathers by a fire in a shelter on the plains. There were five of us siblings, and we all piled on top of each other as puppies tend to do.

It was winter on The Earth Mother and very cold outside, but it was warm and wonderful inside the mud and wooden hut that housed all of us. The Hu-mans who lived with us were called Ni-U-Ku-Skam, which meant "water people."

When my eyes first opened, the initial Hu-man I saw was Miniya, who I knew right away was Mia from my past Life. Her elders say her name means "she who will do great things." I wondered how they could possibly know that, but these were Hu-mans who had a genuine connection with The Earth Mother, so they tended to be very intuitive.

I became Miniya's favorite pup, as she seemed to know I was Puck from her prior Life. We gazed into each other's eyes a lot, and she often sang the songs of her pack to me. She named me Odakota, which meant "friend," but I will always be Puck, as it is the name given to me by The Most High, and it's what Azul calls me as well.

～ ～

Summer set in, and Miniya trained me so I could help transport things her Hu-mans needed to take with them. Since I was still a puppy, she made me a tiny sleeve to pull. I felt proud because she let me haul a few of her Hu-man mother's pots alongside grown-up Dog who pulled heavier items, such as poles to be used for huts.

We traveled all the way to the plains. These Hu-mans were fun-loving and pure of Spirit. They patted my head to encourage me, and they said that in no time I'd be pulling Miniya behind me since she didn't like to work hard. Everyone laughed at the joke because they loved Miniya and knew just how much she cared for me.

As the moons passed I became the head canine at our new camp, so I got fed first and was allowed to share Miniya's family's hut, which consisted of large animal hides sewn together and called a Tipi. I was indeed proud and contented to serve these Hu-mans.

Our pack, well, tribe as they called it, was similar to what I remembered in my past Life. These tribal Hu-mans sometimes spoke to one another without words, and they respected The Earth Mother in the same way as Dog. All That Is existed to them, too, although they called it The Great Spirit. And they had great trust in how The Earth Mother took care of us all. They understood that the trees and rocks and all the waters possessed memories, and all of this was just as alive as animals. Since our tribe believed that everything possessed a Spirit Life, we had tree Spirits, star Spirits, and animal ancestors, and I learned how to give Honor to all Life in this way as well.

However, I also discovered that even these tribal Hu-mans, good as they were as a whole, didn't always think alike. In this camp, some men insisted on fighting just to fight, while others fought to protect what they owned—or to acquire more. Some of these Hu-mans had forgotten that The Earth Mother existed for everyone to benefit from equally.

There was always enough food and hides to go around, but battles ensued with neighboring tribes, mostly over hunting rights. However, there was no real hatred among these competing Hu-mans, only strong convictions. Rarely did these disagreements end in the loss of Life, and when this occurred both sides grieved. All in all, it was a peaceful Life, and I especially enjoyed it when another kind of Hu-man came to visit.

These Hu-mans were called Frenchmen, and they brought us gifts. Our tribe's Hu-mans liked them even though they were very different. The Frenchmen traded their furs for our baskets and blankets, and they often spent all night singing their songs and playing their music and making us laugh.

These were wonderful times, and we looked forward to their visits, which came at least once every year. Miniya enjoyed spending time with Jean, a big but gentle Frenchman who insisted that she walk with him. I could sense she liked him very much, so it was no surprise to me that Miniya, with me by her side, went off to live with Jean by the river. We were all very happy together, and in the spring the three of us went back to the tribal camp and visited family.

We returned to the river, and the next spring Jean and Miniya had a child together, whom they loved and named Claire. Even with the baby by her side, Miniya never ignored me, and I took on the role of this child's protector, barking proudly that no harm would ever come to this little girl as long as I was around.

It was not long before we were visited by Hu-mans called "white" men. These white Hu-mans seemed to arrive all at once, and my tribal Hu-mans and I ran into them everywhere. They came to trade, and they had Jean and some of his French friends, who also lived by the water, build riverboats for them. They weren't as nice as the French Hu-mans, and they took what they wanted without asking.

One day, as we were preparing for our journey back to Miniya's family's camp, we met up with some Hu-man tribal friends who were traveling from the plains. They told us the news from the past year. They used words like "soldiers" and "reservations" and mentioned a disease called "smallpox." We also learned that some of the nearby tribes now possessed things called "guns." Greed had become an issue, and there was killing, which was referred to as "war."

This news made the French Hu-mans we knew very sad, and they expressed concern for Miniya and Jean and little Claire. By jumping around and acting silly, I tried to make everyone laugh, but I had trouble understanding exactly what was happening and found these gloomy emotions strange and foreign because they were so rare.

Some French Hu-mans insisted on traveling with us to offer protection. They talked about how the white Hu-mans with their rulers, called "governors," were taking our people away and treating them like prisoners. How could we be prisoners in our own homes? No matter, the white Hu-mans informed us that our tribes were going to be placed on reservations to live so that other white Hu-mans could have our land. How could anyone own the land? The land belonged to everyone—and everyone belonged to the land.

I felt danger all around. We carefully but quickly made our way from our river dwelling to Miniya's camp on the plains. On the way, we found several tribal camps destroyed and the native Hu-mans lying dead and scattered on the earth to decay like discarded wood.

I sensed even greater peril as Miniya, Jean, and some French Human friends, who refused to let us travel alone, pressed hurriedly toward the tribal camp on the plains, which, when we arrived, we found burned to the ground!

Miniya's grandparents, as well as most of her other family members, had passed into Spirit. I edged my way among the bodies and noticed that they all had little holes in them. I wondered how such a small thing could take away a Life. More important, I wondered why. Every other Hu-man who'd lived in the village was gone, and we didn't know where.

An eerie loneliness breathed in the silence. Dusty ghosts blew around in the dry wind that coursed through the plain grasses and moaned in such a way that it made me cower. No Hu-man nor Dog need see the dead to know that something terrible had happened here.

The Hu-mans placed the bodies on a burial platform made of long branches and hides so that The Great Spirit could see the dead clearly from The Father Sky. We stayed for three days in mourning. Jean comforted Miniya the best he could, and I spent my time with little Claire, allowing her to climb on me and tug at my ears and tail. I was troubled, not only by the overpowering stench of death but by a vile odor I remembered from my past. It was a smell that haunted me: the smell of Hazz.

Miniya cried a lot in the days that followed, but she looked to me for the strength to carry on. She talked to me as if I were a Hu-man, saying that she wanted to be more like me. I told her in my way to live each day as it presented itself and not to dwell in the past. The "now" was the only reality we had on The Earth Mother.

She would sometimes sing to me, her voice high and pure, letting me know that she understood exactly what I was saying by the words she sang. I joined in once in a while, throwing my head back and howling to her sounds. That made her laugh, and my Heart swelled with pride and Love for her.

We left the plains and traveled far up into the mountains to live. We were happy there, and Miniya kept busy making a cozy home for us. Our French Hu-man friends came to visit when the weather allowed, always bringing news from the plains. Unfortunately, most of the time the information was unpleasant and Miniya would start crying. But we felt safe in our mountain home, which was a sturdy cabin with a strong door.

— —

The day started out much as all the rest, Miniya and I collecting eggs from our chickens. My Hu-man had a big belly because she was going to give us another child, so I had to carry the basket for her and stay close by.

When we approached our cabin, strangers on horseback, along with many animals pulling wagons, came into our yard. Jean left the house to talk to these Hu-mans. Maybe he would ask them to stay for a meal, since on this morning we had lots of eggs. But I soon sensed something wasn't right, and the hair bristled across my back. Perhaps these were the "soldiers" we'd been warned about.

Instinct told me to stop walking, and I dropped the basket full of eggs when I heard the blast. It sounded like thunder, and I caught a harsh scent I'd never smelled before and took off running as fast as I could into the yard, only to find that Jean had fallen and was bleeding from his chest.

I leaped and grabbed a Hu-man with my teeth. I tasted him; smelled him: Hazz. But he was fast to put me down with a swipe of something hard in his hand, which temporarily knocked me out. When I regained my senses I heard Miniya screaming. In a wobbly state, I ran to her.

Hu-mans, all dressed alike, had bound her hands and feet with a rope. She struggled mightily, especially considering her condition, but to no avail. I began frantically running in circles, when I heard little Claire cry from inside our cabin. I turned to go to her just as a foul-smelling Hu-man came outside our home with the baby in his arms— and took Claire's Life by stabbing her with a long knife. He dropped her tiny body next to Jean's, smiling as he did so.

Miniya was thrown into a wagon covered in hides, and these unbe-lievably cruel Hu-mans left hurriedly while I was still trying to figure out what had happened. My mind reeled in pain from the blow to my head, and my thinking was slow and murky. My own blood blinded me in my right eye. I fell next to Jean and Claire. I howled in anguish that I had failed to protect them as Dog, in particular, Claire, whom I had vowed to protect no matter the peril.

I learned that what I had done to Hazz in my past Life was the same as what these men had done to us. They took Life for no reason except out of hatred. The mirror Azul had told me to look into reflected exactly what was clear and true: fear and hate were the substance of that which we don't understand.

Since I hadn't been of any service to Jean and Claire, I had to try to protect Miniya the best I could. I followed her trail all day, until the sol-diers stopped at a fenced-in area with big buildings inside. Hu-mans in their strange clothing, which I heard someone call "uniforms," dragged Miniya from the wagon and put her in with other Hu-mans, whom a solder referred to as "our people." Our people! I lay down outside the fence that encircled the camp and listened to the conversations.

Jean was killed because he lived with Miniya, who was, as these Humans called her, "an Indian." And they took little Claire's Life because she was what they referred to as a "half-breed." These Humans had captured "our people" and brought them to this place so we could be sent, together, to a reservation far away. At no point during the daylight that followed could I see Miniya, but I had her full scent and heard her screams. Her agony made me ill.

When morning came, all the Indians were tied together with leather straps and walked in a single line between the soldiers' horses. I had permanently lost my sight in the eye Hazz had struck, but my other eye was fine, as was my sense of smell, so I managed to come to Miniya during the first night. She held me tightly and would not let go as she cried into my fur.

With my licks and whimpers I showed her how glad I was to see her, and how sorry I was for not being able to save Jean and little Claire. She knew exactly the message I wanted to convey, and she whispered over and over to me, "It was not your fault, it was not your fault." I didn't agree.

I was allowed to walk beside Miniya during the next day, and I did so in silence out of respect for her grief. But at night, when were supposed to sleep, we "talked" until dawn. I told her not to feel sad about what had happened, that Life itself was a Plan far greater than what we understood, and to have faith in The Great Spirit. I told her, in time, all would be as it should be. I wasn't sure if she accepted what I said, since I was very confused about what was happening around us, but I told her again and again that our Love would see us through.

I lapped her face and said, "I'm devoted to you, Miniya, and there is nothing we can't endure together. I still have one good eye. Maybe we'll find another French Hu-man like Jean, and you will have another Claire. Remember, Miniya, Love is all that matters." Her tears told me that she believed otherwise.

On our journey, to where I didn't know, we passed thousands of freshly skinned buffalo, with the hides and much meat left to rot in the sun. It was beyond reason why any Hu-man would waste such a wonderful gift that The Great Spirit had provided for everyone's survival.

Two weeks into our trek, we paused on a hilltop that overlooked a great battleground. I watched hundreds of Hu-mans pass into Spirit as one huge cloud rose into the sky. I wondered if they were going to a Bridge like the one I went to at the end of my Life here on The Earth Mother. I contemplated whether Hu-mans had a Home like mine. I hoped they indeed did.

On the third week into our long walk, Miniya was ready to have her baby. Some brave Indians, who were from our home tribe, convinced the soldiers to wait where we were until she gave birth. Only a few of us were allowed to stay with her, and I remained by her side to offer whatever I could of Love and comfort.

Her newborn son arrived with the help of some Indian females, but Miniya, who was in great distress throughout the birth, confided in one woman who was a longtime friend. Miniya told her about little Claire and Jean and begged her to send this baby to The Great Spirit. She told her friend she wanted the baby to know hands that were kind and understanding, rather than subject him to the white soldiers' evil.

Miniya believed that the soldiers would either kill or corrupt this child because of his mixed blood. Miniya was beside herself with grief, and the Indians with us shared her pain, certain she was right. They said they had all heard what Life was like for Indian children who'd been allowed to survive. When old enough, these boys and girls had been sent away to white man's schools and their Indian Spirits stolen. None of the females in our tribe would want a child of hers brought up in the white man's world.

I remembered what Azul had said to me, and I relayed her words to Miniya: "You must let your baby live. A Hu-man's Heart can change in an instant if it's touched with pure Love from All That Is." I whined and pawed at her arm to emphasize what I was saying. "Azul told me that not one Soul is lost forever, and that everyone comes into each Life with a special Plan that needs to be lived out. So you must have Faith. How do you know this baby, who will grow to be a half-white, half-Indian man, won't be the one Hu-man who stops hatred? Your son might become a leader who brings all tribes together in Peace." My story went to deaf ears. Miniya was emphatic in her resolve, and the women agreed with her, taking the baby away.

I stayed with my Miniya and agonized over how I could be such a terrible teacher. This Life was happening far too fast for me. I wasn't young Dog anymore, and Life up until a few weeks ago was almost as good as being Home. I wasn't prepared for all this sudden sadness.

That night Miniya had calmed down, and she searched my face as she gently stroked the fur on my head. I heard her sweet voice tell me she loved me: "Odakota, you have been a good friend and teacher. I want you to know that I am in the place you have always prepared me for. The place in my Heart that has no past pain. I give all bad things that are happening to our people to The Great Spirit. I do this because I know that all will be well in time. Dear Odakota, I'm at Peace now and going to join Jean and Claire and the baby just born, which I know is in Spirit too. May The Great Spirit give you two good eyes on the other side so you can find me and . . ."

Like the fast mist climbing the hills after a rain, Miniya passed away just as quickly. The women who'd attended Miniya told everyone that the baby was born dead and that Miniya had died in childbirth, but of course she'd died of a broken Heart.

Hazz put an end to my journey soon after Miniya passed into Spirit. He said he didn't want a dog like me around, and I was oddly grateful that he came along with my death on his mind. I wanted to go Home anyway.

— ∽

In silence, my angel and I walk the lush pastures of Summerland. She's aware that this past Life has been hard on me, and I have to believe this is why she doesn't push me now. I'm thinking that Hazz's taking my Life has evened the score between him and me. But since Azul offers no comment on the subject, I take her silence as a sign that my relationship with Hazz isn't over.

"I think I failed miserably," I blurt without provocation. "Miniya and I just lived for the moment. Sure, we had a good Life, all of us including the French Hu-man, until that fateful day. And when I told Miniya at the end to have Faith, to believe and trust in The Great Spirit's Plan, she didn't want to fight for the future—for herself or her baby. She let everything go. I tried . . . but I didn't teach her a thing." I could not help but whimper at my defeat.

"Oh, Puck, you are so wrong," Azul says in a most gentle tone. "You taught her a great lesson without knowing it. It is called Acceptance."

I frown. "Miniya's actions didn't seem to me very *accepting*."

Azul strokes my head as we stop and look over a lake. "Acceptance sometimes is just letting go and trusting All That Is."

I say, "She sent her baby away to be killed without accepting that maybe he could have been the one to change everything."

"That was her decision," Azul replies, her voice remaining soft. "Miniya knew she was going to die. She didn't want to leave her child behind to face what would likely be great unhappiness. Right or wrong, it was her choice of what she thought would be for the child's Highest Good. Remember, Miniya had a Plan, just like all beings. Know that your words will stay with her, and in another Lifetime she will recognize the value of what you said about her son's being the one who will bring about change." She strokes me gently. "Now, dear Puck, rest and relish the joy of being at Home. There is still much work to be done, so take pleasure in the Peace while Here."

7

ydia Rose raised a flour-dusted black hand to shield her tired brown eyes from the bright afternoon sun. She searched the street outside the kitchen window as she paused from her baking. "Where is that boy?" she whispered so softly it would be inaudible but to her. It wasn't like Mitchell to be late from school. She was hounded with worry every afternoon at this time. The year was 1928, and the world wasn't a kind place for Negro families in this barebones community appropriately called "Shanty Town"—even on a map. Mitchell had insisted that she allow him to walk home from school alone, afraid the other kids would mock him about being with his mother. After all, *he* was eleven years old now. Yes, she had to let go, but her boy's walking by himself filled her with anxiety. She continued her baking, kneading the dough and adding an impatient slap now and then.

She'd just popped dough in the oven when she heard a group of loud boys talking outside her small porch. Mitchell was in the middle of the kids, being jostled and taunted by one of the older boys, who demanded, "Leave us have 'im, Mitchell! We found 'im! Gimme 'im here or I'll kick you into tomorrow!"

Lydia Rose opened the screen door and called down to everyone, her voice strong and menacing: "What y'all got going on out there?

Mitchell, git inside right now, and the rest of y'all git your black behinds down the road!"

"But, Mama—" Mitchell started to argue.

"Don't give me any lip, Boy! You get yourself in here right now or you gonna regret it plenty! Now!" The other kids moved a few steps back from Mitchell, but they hooted and poked their feet at a small hound on the end of a frayed piece of dirty clothesline one of the boys was holding. Mitchell stood his ground against his mother's words. His eyes were big and round, his bottom lip trembling. Lydia sensed something more going on, so she looked past him to what was now a rather rowdy bunch of kids.

She called out to them, "What y'all got there?" Nobody spoke as Mitchell approached his mother.

"Mama, I found this li'l ol' puppy dog under the school porch last week, and I been feeding him and takin' good care of him, and I didn't want to tell you 'cause you get so mad all the time, and then these boys took him from me and they plan to hurt him, I just know. Please, please, Mama." The words tumbled out of her son's mouth in such a rush that Lydia was surprised at the passion they carried; Mitchell was shy and all too quiet most of the time. She had never seen him this upset. He was clearly fighting back tears, and Lydia was moved by the sight of her young son in such an agitated state. She grabbed a broom from beside the door and seemed to fly off the porch. She swung the broom wildly in the direction of the boys, and they backed up.

"Y'all git away from that dog now, you boys hear! That dog belong to Mitchell! I'll blister your behinds now, and don't think I can't." Lydia pointed the broom handle at the largest boy in the group. "And if'n I can't, Buster Jones, sure 'nough your daddy will have a plenty good reason to whup you when I tell him 'bout this!"

Buster Jones, at the mention of his name, brought the dog forward. The boy's shoulders sank noticeably as he spoke to Mitchell, "Here's your dumb mutt." Then to Lydia, "Please don't say nothin' to my daddy, Miz Lydia. We was just funnin' around." The other boys cursed and spit in disgust at this declaration from Buster, who slunk away and soon began trotting off. She glared at the rest of the kids, who one by one turned and left.

Once the boys were out of earshot, Lydia spun around to Mitchell, her fists firm against her hips. "What is in that head a yours, Boy! You can't bring dat dog in dis here house. What do ya think we can feed 'im with when we can barely feed ourselves? What on earth was you thinkin'? Here you come home and take me away from my bakin' to fight your fights for you, and then ya bring me more bad times, fo' sure! Leave dat dirty, mangy animal go, then git yourself in this here house. Go on, now, leave 'im loose."

Lydia went into the house to check on the bread, and when she came outside to find out if Mitchell had done what she'd told him to do, he was sitting on the porch steps, the puppy cradled in his arms. Lydia's Heart softened at the sight of her son like this. He was so alone all the time. Life was hard for all the dark folks now, and it looked to be harder on Mitchell because of the passive way he viewed things. She had wanted to raise him to be a fighter, to protect himself and take care of his needs in this violent world. But Mitchell was different. He constantly posed questions about segregation and why his people were so poor; questions she couldn't answer without blistering anger. Lydia had good reason to be upset.

Eleven years previously, a recently pregnant Lydia, along with her husband and both their extended families, migrated to Illinois from Georgia to find a better Life that they'd heard existed in the north. Unemployment, and the poverty that always came with it, had made moving the only way to improve their sad set of circumstances. And in addition to jobs, there was supposed to be some degree of racial equality, as in the south racial tensions had made Life dangerous for all African-Americans.

Lydia's husband was hired in February of 1917 by The Aluminum Ore Company, located in East St. Louis, Illinois. He and other black men were hired to replace striking white workers, although at a lower wage than their Caucasian counterparts. The hiring didn't sit well with the whites on strike, who were already inflamed, and they made their added discontent known. Yet despite the unrest Lydia could see a glimmer of hope for a good future for the baby she would bring into the world. It wasn't long before that dream ended.

In May, white workers complained to the mayor's office about black workers taking their jobs, and at lower wages. Before long riots broke out everywhere in the city. Lydia's husband was pulled from a trolley and beaten to death, and soon the lynching of black men became commonplace.

Fearful for her own Life, and for that of her unborn baby, Lydia and a few of her neighbors moved to a more rural part of Illinois. In July, word reached them that full-blown mob rule was rampant in their old neighborhood. White men had set fire to homes and shot black residents as they ran into the street. The National Guard, which had been called out to protect the black communities, paid little heed to the plight of the Negroes, essentially turning their backs. The country was again embroiled in intense racial turmoil and injustice.

For weeks after that news, Lydia mourned along with other new residents of the small, poor community where they'd settled. Mitchell was born in August, and the women of Shanty Town gave Lydia all the loving support they could muster.

Although everyone in this black settlement was dirt poor and often hungry, each person clung to the other and created a mighty strength overall. A church for the black families was the first order of business, then a school was started for the black children. A community market with shared produce from the nearby farms that hired black men began operating, and the women found employment as domestic help at the estate houses that dotted the countryside. Lydia worked as a seamstress, walking miles with Mitchell to pick up items needing mending, which she completed at home and often returned the next day. At times she would do the washing and ironing in the basement of a grand home while baby Mitchell played on the floor beside her.

When Mitchell came of school age, she walked with him on her way to work and met up with him on her return trip. Most black school children were taught only enough reading, writing and arithmetic to get by.

Lydia herself could not read or write, so when the new reverend of their church offered to tutor some of the children in further education, she pushed Mitchell to the front of the line.

Her son was exceptionally curious and naturally smart, so it wasn't long before he showed himself to be a cut above everyone else. Regardless, she worried herself into many sleepless nights because of what his future might bring. There was no safe place for people of color, and even educated white men and women could be seething segregationists.

Today, sitting with his little rescued mutt in his arms, eleven-year-old Mitchell bothered her in a way like never before. She was so shaken to see her son this distraught that she sat down beside him. Her voice broke as she said, "Mitchell, what we really gonna to do wid a dog?"

Mitchell's eyes got big. "Mama, I can take care of him. He won't be no trouble at all, I promise. I been gettin' scraps from the butcher man. I can't explain it, but this dog knows me. He picked me, not me him." Mitchell stroked the puppy's head, adding proudly, "Mama, he be protectin' us too."

Lydia ran her fingers through Mitchell's curly dark-brown hair before getting to her feet. "Lord a-mighty, Mitchell, you gonna be the death of me yet. So, whacha gonna name him, Boy?" She looked at me suspiciously. "I ain't never seen such a poorly lookin' pup. Glory be."

Lydia chuckled and shook her head as she went inside her small shack, letting the screen door pop closed behind her. Mitchell repeated what his mother had just said. He hollered into the house, "His name gonna be Glory Be, Mama. That's right, Glory Be." He smacked his lips and said to himself, "I got me a puppy."

Mitchell smiled and buried his face in my neck, unaware of the white streak of flour his mama had left in his hair. I raised my head and licked Mitchell's face, loving the sound of his laughter that followed.

What Mitchell had said was true, I did pick him, although it threw me that Mia and Miniya in my past Life was now a boy named Mitchell. I also didn't mind that he called me Glory Be. I was just happy to be with him, so long as he knew, on some level, that I was Puck. I was pretty sure he didn't understand why he was drawn to me, but I had it down quite well. Lessons were to be learned and taught, and I was up for the challenge.

It wasn't long before I was curled up beside Mitchell's bed at night and going off to school with him every morning. I think it gave Lydia peace of mind to know that Mitchell wasn't alone while she worked. I helped Mitchell make friends, running around the schoolyard while other children laughed and chased me. It occurred to me that I was not only teaching Mitchell the lessons of Dog, but I was touching many other young boys and girls as well. I was spreading the Spirit of Joy, and it felt wonderful. There was a lot of pain and sadness in these dark-skinned children, and I was making Life happier for them.

Not wanting to brag, but I noticed that my mere presence uplifted the Spirits of most everyone in Shanty Town. And during the next five years I became a common sight everywhere in our little community. People knew my name, and these kind Negroes patted my head and talked to me as if I could change things for them. Everyone needed comfort in those days. There was something going on called "The Great Depression," and it made people very sad. I did what I could to improve their dispositions. As for Mitchell, my devotion to him was evident in every way. He was my Hu-man, and I loved him as much as he loved me, and despite becoming pretty hungry at times, we were happy.

—◆ ◆—

Mitchell's sixteenth birthday arrived. Lydia Rose opened the oven door, took the sugar cake she had just made, and set it on the porch railing to cool. She'd saved a bunch of little sugar cubes that she'd *borrowed* from her employer's sugar bowl that sat on the sideboard in the dining room.

Thankfully, she was still employed by the family she had known for years. They loved Lydia and watched Mitchell grow up before their eyes. They even made a place for me to stay on their back porch some rainy days, as I was always tagging along. And even though they had escaped the loss of their money in "The Crash," they had warned Lydia that the day was fast approaching when they might have to let her go.

But on this day everything was Life as usual. Lydia wiped her hands on her apron and squinted into the hot August morning sun, which hung over Shanty Town like the primary image in a watercolor painting and promised clear and peaceful weather.

Her cooking finished for a while, Lydia picked up her sewing kit and some linen and settled into her old rocker and began humming her favorite spiritual. I'd heard it often and knew it well. It soothed me as I lay at Mitchell's feet just as his best friend, Owen, joined us.

Mitchell and Owen had finished high school together that spring, and they talked about going off somewhere to another school to learn new things. Owen thought a lot like Mitchell. They often spent their evenings discussing what they called "civil rights" and reading articles, when they could get them, about leading black figures.

Owen's father made a fair living as a trumpet player in Chicago and wasn't home much. But when he did come back to Shanty Town, everyone wanted to hear all the news and happenings in "The Windy City," as folks called it. Since the 1920s, black musicians played the "blues" and black performers flourished in the theater. There were laws enacted that protected blacks from discrimination, but marauding packs of white men called the Ku Klux Klan still existed and struck terror into the Hearts of small-town black communities.

Owen and Mitchell soon had dreams of going to Chicago; dreams of going to what they called "The University of Chicago." I got the feeling I wasn't included in this Plan, and it concerned me. I rolled over and looked up at Mitchell. I loved him so much. He was young in Hu-man years, but he was very smart and I could sense how good he felt when talking of equality and listening to people he called "humanitarians."

"Glory," he whispered to me one night as I closed my eyes, "I'm going to be a lawyer one day. I'm going to help my people live free. I'm going to be the one who brings all people together as one. Like Reverend Davis says, 'We are all God's Children, and He doesn't see color, just Souls all trying their best to get along in this world.' I believe there's a Plan for us black folk, Glory, and it's for all of us to be free of discrimination and united as one." I had no idea what being a lawyer meant, but

I thought it had something to do with helping people know right from wrong.

Lydia was very proud of her son, and she often told him that he was the hope of their people. She was always saying that times were much better for him now; much improved from when she was his age. Still, she worried about him. Me, I lived Life to Life. And at this time—in my current Life—all was going along well for me as Dog. In truth, only the present was real for me, as the past was gone and the future didn't exist yet. This wasn't Dog Law, it was Universal Law. It seemed to me that everyone should know this, yet it amazed me that most Hu-mans didn't have a clue about these realities.

Dust rose off the dry road that led into Shanty Town, and we all looked up to see a car bouncing through the ruts. I immediately picked up the engine's sound and knew who was inside the vehicle, so I jumped in happy circles, barking my welcome. Mrs. James, Lydia's employer, and Melody, her only daughter, had come to visit.

They waved a merry hello as they ambled up the path to our house. Melody held a large woven basket. "Lord-a-mighty!" Lydia's voice rang out. "What brings you good people all the way over here?" Lydia smiled. "If I knew y'all was comin', I woulda finished Miz Melody's dress sooner." She held up the sewing she was working on.

"Oh, forget about that for now, Lydia," Mrs. James said, her sweet voice rising. "We're not here for that! We've come to drop off some things for you, and to wish Mitchell a happy birthday!"

The strong scents of delicious foods had long overtaken me, and Mrs. James took a sugary biscuit from the basket and gave it to me, saying, "For you, Glory, our ever-gallant ambassador of good will." This nice Hu-man crouched down and looked into my eyes. She always smelled like the flowers in the fields we passed on our way to her huge house. I couldn't resist, and I gave her a big lick on her nose and everyone laughed. While they did this I gobbled down my biscuit and ran my tongue around my mouth. I'd almost forgotten what rich treats tasted like, it had been so long since I'd had any.

Mrs. James took the basket from Melody and passed it on to Lydia, who smiled wide with delight at the gift of food. "Lord-a-mighty, we thanks you so much."

Mrs. James sighed. "I wish it could be more, Lydia, but times are hard all over. But much harder for you folks down here than us, so we want to share with you." She sighed again. "I'm wondering how much longer these bad times are going to stay with us."

Lydia's eyes filled up with tears, as happens to Hu-mans when they feel things in their Hearts. Her voice trembled as she said, "Blessed be, Miz James. I thanks you so much. We all does."

Mrs. James reached into a large plaid bag she carried and said to Mitchell, "I know you've been talking about going to college one day soon, so this is for you, young man." She laid a coat and matching trousers in Mitchell's arms. "It's one of my husband suits he grew too big to wear anymore, so we figured you might like it. Your mama will have to make it fit you, but I think you'll look just fine in it." She winked at Mitchell. "And quite handsome, too." She patted Mitchell's chest to make her point.

Melody said shyly, "Mitchell, I know this is being handed down to you, but it would make my whole family proud if you'd accept it."

Mitchell only nodded, but I could sense my Hu-man's Heart beating faster. Sometimes, on the way back from school, Melody would meet up with Mitchell and me, and we'd all go down to the swimming hole and they'd throw sticks for me to swim after. These two were close friends, but I felt they didn't want anyone to know this for some reason. For me, I loved being with them, as their Hearts were pure and their laughter always like music. Afterwards, Melody would skip on home in the opposite direction from the way we walked, and Mitchell normally sang all the back to Shanty Town.

Today was a wonderful day. Mrs. James sat on the porch and talked to Lydia as Mitchell and Melody walked out to the road behind the house. I ambled along behind him and half-listened to the two friends as they chattered about things I could not care less about. Suddenly, our path was blocked by a filthy pickup truck. Two men stepped from the truck and leaned against its bed. Both men chewed on long thin pieces of grass and stared at us.

One man, with big yellow teeth, said to the other, "Well, how 'bout it, Henry? I do believe that there dog looks like one of your hounds that went missing last month." Then to Mitchell, "Boy, where'd you get that hound? You steal that dog?"

Mitchell drew up to his full size, which really wasn't very big, as he was a bit smallish for his age. "No, sir. I didn't steal anything from anybody. This here is my dog. I've had him since he was a pup. Everyone around here will tell you that."

I raised the hackles on my neck hair and growled loud and long. The strong odor of gas from the truck had covered a smell I now recognized all too well: the smell of Hazz! So here he was again, and his new name was Henry!

The Hu-man with yellow teeth said, "Seems to me, Henry, this boy is lyin'. That sure 'nough is your dog."

"I believe you're right, Matthew," Henry said as he narrowed his eyes on Melody and said to her, "but right now I'm interested in what a pretty li'l thing like this is doin' down here in a hole like Shanty Town. Girl, your mama know you're keepin' this kinda company?"

It was Melody who rose up this time. "She does. She's visiting with our seamstress right now. And Mitchell is my friend. Now get out of our way."

Henry pushed the straw hat he wore to the back of his head and whistled. "My, my. We got us a little spitfire here, don't we? You Dan James's girl, ain't you? And didn't your daddy just give a speech at the town hall last month about civil rights or some such garbage? You can tell him for me, little girl, he's barking up the wrong tree."

"Tell him yourself, if you're man enough," Melody said. "Now, get out of our way."

I was surprised at Melody's standing up to these men, but Henry acted unfazed as he reached in the back of the truck and grabbed a rope and came at us.

I barked, Melody screamed, and Mitchell hung onto my hind quarters and shouted for me to back away. I didn't obey; I couldn't help myself. I lunged at my Lifetime adversary. My teeth sank deep into his calf muscle, and Henry howled. I would have given my Life to protect Mitchell. I hadn't bitten Henry out of hate; it was in self-defense. I remembered what Azul had said.

Henry cursed and looped the rope around my neck, pulling me toward the truck. The other man held a big stick and started to beat me. I jumped around, snapping furiously until foam flew from my mouth. I heard Mitchell pleading. Then I heard another voice, and Mrs. James rushed from her car.

"Release that dog immediately!" she demanded. "Release him, I say!" Matthew backed off but Henry still held the rope, which was now so tight around my neck it choked me.

"Mrs. James, with all due respect," Henry said, the pressure still on my neck, "this ain't none a your business. This boy stole one a my coon dogs, and I'm taking him back. That's my right, ain't it?"

"You have no rights here," Mrs. James said, her voice cracking. "Release that dog immediately or I will call the sheriff. I have known that dog for years, and he does not belong to you. This is the boy's dog."

Henry spit. "The dog has a bad attitude. Probably from living here in Shanty Town." Henry released the rope and Mitchell loosened it from my neck and tossed it aside. I collapsed and Mitchell rubbed my sore neck.

Henry said, "Mind if I ask you, Mrs. James, what you're doing here?"

"Yes, I do mind, as it clearly is none of your business. However, my intentions here are far more honorable than yours, no doubt." She waved her finger at both men. "Don't come here looking for trouble. Leave these people alone. You understand?"

Henry tilted his head toward us and sneered. "Well, Mrs. James, I'd keep a closer eye on this here daughter of yours—and her choice of friends."

Mrs. James raised her voice in a way that caused even me to cower. "How dare you! Leave this place at once! Get out of here! Both of you! Get out!"

They left, and Mrs. James gave us a ride back to where Lydia and some neighbors waited anxiously. Apparently many folks had heard the commotion. Lydia ran to Mitchell and hugged him tightly. I wondered why she was so upset. I mean, everything was fine now; yet I sensed real fear in Lydia. Apparently this wasn't about Henry stealing me, as there was something much deeper going on that I didn't understand.

What I could understand was my encounter with Henry. He'd remembered me! I was sure of this because his hatred for me was unmistakable. Yes, undeniable hatred. If he had been successful in taking me, he would no doubt have beaten me to death. Henry was not a good man. Azul had told me that all Hu-mans were basically good, they just had things happen in their individual Plans that sometimes turned them toward darkness, and a man could change in a heartbeat. Somehow, I had trouble believing this about Henry. How was I ever going to free him from himself—and enable him to live the Lesson that would free me as well? Really?

I attempted to make sense of Life and death, and it seems that all of us return to Life to try to undo the wrongs of the past. If our journey is toward good, we will want to keep on this Path, because a wrongdoing such as my killing Hazz will come back again and again until it's rectified in some way. I figured this out all by myself, from watching and listening. I must ask Azul if I'm right.

Mitchell's "new" suit was draped over a chair so he could see his clothes while he ate his huge birthday meal. For me, there was a big raw meaty bone that I recklessly gnawed under the table. I was as contented as I have ever been.

— —

September was upon us, and it ushered in the promise of Owen's traveling to visit his father in Chicago, with Mitchell going along. Mitchell talked to me about this, and I tried to understand why I was to stay and look after Lydia. I loved her, but I wanted to be with Mitchell, and his leaving me was like a little piece of my Heart departing with him as well.

But this afternoon, Mitchell was to meet Melody after her school day ended. They'd planned on a walk down by the swimming hole at the river while I played fetch with them. I assumed that they'd talk about Mitchell's upcoming adventure in Chicago with Owen. Melody still had a year of high school remaining, and if Mitchell went to The University of Chicago I was certain she'd miss spending time with him.

We arrived at our normal spot but Melody wasn't there yet, so Mitchell sat on a tree that had fallen partway over the water. He dropped bits of bark into the gentle current and waited. Quite a while passed and Melody still hadn't shown up, so Mitchell told me that something must have happened to keep her away. We took a walk up the riverbank and toward the white side of town in hope of seeing her coming our way, smiling and giggling as she always did whenever we got together. But she was nowhere to be found, and we kept walking.

The fall days had become shorter, and it wasn't long before a murky dusk wrapped around us. If we continued on we wouldn't be able to make it home until after dark, so we had no choice but to go back. Mitchell threw one last stick down the path for me to chase, and when I grabbed it in my mouth and spun around to him, several men were rapidly trying to surround him, each one holding something in his hands.

Mitchell started to walk backwards as I charged full force into the circle of men, barking and biting at whoever was closest. I couldn't see their faces, as their heads and upper bodies were covered by burlap feed bags, but I recognized one Hu-man's scent all too well, and it was accompanied by the stink of hate and fear.

I attacked as if diseased by madness, but I was no match for this many Hu-mans. The Hu-man whose smell I knew looped a chain around my neck and drew it up so tight I could hardly breathe. This Hu-man took something hard and black from under his burlap cover and put it to my head. "Someone ought to shoot this dog," he said, "and it might as well be me. Shut him up for good."

A man shouted, "Henry, put that gun away. If you shoot that damn dog, all of Shanty Town will be down on us. Tie him to that tree over there and forget about him. We got business here. Let's get on with it."

I jerked with all my strength against the chain that now held me to a tree trunk. My neck bled as the chain cut through my flesh until it reached bone. I barked as loud as I ever had. I barked for Azul to come to help; I barked for any Hu-man to help; I barked for anything to help.

The men took Mitchell farther down the path toward the river's edge, and I heard them talking. They said Melody's name. Beautiful, sweet Melody. It wasn't long before Mitchell screamed once; a short, shrill yell at the top of his lungs. Silence followed as the men rushed away. I barked for so long and loud that I was left with only a whimper of noise from my throat.

My fur was matted thick with blood, and I had trouble catching my breath, when from out of nowhere I caught the scent of Owen, who ran up and untied me. Soon, all of Shanty Town's residents who could walk were at the river. Lydia, who was among the first to arrive, fell to her knees, screaming, wailing to her God. I had no thoughts, only dull feelings of what had just happened to my Hu-man—whom I was to protect.

Several males hoisted Mitchell in their arms and made their way to our house. Owen carried me, as I was too weak from blood loss and exhaustion to walk on my own. The women sang mournful songs as the men laid Mitchell on our kitchen table. They sang as they washed his body, their grief rocking them back and forth. Lydia was held close by the other women, as all she could do was sob and say she wanted to be with her son.

They dressed him in the suit that was to herald in a whole new world for him. Mitchell looked wonderful to me. I nuzzled his hand, which was still warm, but he wasn't there with me. All night long we sang and rocked, rocked and sang, our Hearts broken. I understand what Hu-man grief is now, as I'd never felt it with Mia or Miniya.

In the morning, the men brought a wooden box and laid Mitchell inside it. They carried him through town to an overgrown field where I sensed other black people lay in the ground. We sang, we cried, we gave in to our rage, we missed him already.

Owen stood and addressed the crowd as he pulled me to a sitting position beside him. I only half-listened to what Owen said as my eyes were riveted on the hole in which my Mitchell now slept forever while on this Earth. Owen spoke in a loud but calm voice. He talked about justice being the Lord's and how we must not lower ourselves to be like the men who did this to Mitchell. He talked about Love, Acceptance, Forgiveness; the principles Mitchell would have championed if he had lived; the things he'd learned from me.

Then I felt him. My beloved Mitchell was here. And when I turned my head I saw him clearly as he stood beside me; so handsome, smiling and reaching his hand out to pat my fur. I stood on all fours, wagged my tail, and barked at him. Everyone witnessed my actions. Some cried and some shouted hallelujah. Did these Hu-mans see him too?

Mitchell spoke softly so only I could hear him. He's happy that he's now in a wonderful place. There's a Bridge, angels, and good Hu-mans he'd known from his Life on Earth, all excited to see him. Yes, there was my answer: Hu-mans have a Home just like Dog. A Bridge between Here and There. A place of happiness and rest. He told me to be happy and that we'll meet again, and the next time we'll walk and play together forever. After this he vanished, but his smile stayed with me for all the rest of my Life on Earth.

I spent the next four years lying across Mitchell's grave. I didn't want to leave this spot, as there wasn't anything for me in this Life without my Hu-man. Lydia brought me food and water every day, and in winter she took me home with her. But I always returned when I could to be with Mitchell. The people in town talked about me, and soon Hu-mans from great distances away learned of my devotion to this wonderful, gentle young man and the causes he stood for.

Owen visited the grave quite often, staying with me for long periods. He talked to me as if I were Hu-man and constantly patted my head and caressed me. He told me that I was an inspiration for the columns he wrote for a Chicago newspaper. He said it was me who taught his people the value of Peace in devotion to a cause.

The people of Shanty Town grew stronger because of me and Mitchell. That made me feel good. Then one night, as I lay looking out over Mitchell's gravestone, the starlight grew bright in the winter sky.

And although I'd been shivering in the cold I suddenly felt warm and full of energy. Azul appeared to me, her arms open and welcoming. I whimpered to Azul about how much I missed Mitchell. She gathered me to her and said, "You will be with him again soon." I closed my eyes and breathed in the sweet smell of Summerland. I was grateful this Lifetime on Earth was finally over.

8

"What took so long for me to come Home?" I ask Azul as soon as my head clears.

"The Plan, Puck. You had to stay and bring awareness to a very important part of history. I'm very proud of you. Donations came from all over, and Hu-mans erected a monument to you in Shanty Town, with the story of you and Mitchell engraved on a plaque at its base. And because of Mitchell's death, sad as it was, new laws were written to protect all people of color on the Earth. I'm very aware that this past Life on Earth was very hard on you, but everyone at The Bridge is in awe of what you accomplished."

"I really don't understand why my Hu-man was killed during my last Life on Earth."

Azul motions for me to walk with her, and we amble through tall grass to a clear brook I know quite well. "Those men who accosted you and Melody on the road on Mitchell's birthday were out to cause trouble. Of course Henry was Hazz, and he was set on killing you. Everyone who's in a new Life does not remember past Lives, but as you learned, on some level they do have some sense of the past, and Hazz wanted to balance the wrong you did to him.

"When Melody's mother arrived on the scene, Henry and Matthew were outraged that she was defending the people of Shanty Town. That same night, they and their friends burned a cross on the James's lawn to protest the family's sympathy with the black population. And after Mitchell's murder they left their estate in fear for their lives."

"But why did these evil Hu-mans care about Melody?"

"They were afraid of the possibility of mixed bloodlines. It takes light to dispel the darkness. Sadly, sometimes it comes at a steep price."

I had to pause to think. "I just don't understand hate, Azul. I killed Hazz out of hate for an evil Hu-man, but I don't know where that came from . . . or why. Why did those soldiers take Miniya and the other Indians to a different place after killing so many of their people? And since Hazz already took my Life as a Balance for my taking his, why would he want to kill me again? Why do people hate each other so much? Why do they hate someone because of skin color, or the way a person likes to live, or because people believe in different things? Why is this so?"

Azul stops walking and we both sit. "Puck, hate is not the correct word. The proper word is fear. I've listened to you discuss this somewhat with yourself in the past, so let me take it a step further. Hu-mans have become very insecure in their ability to live in God's graces. They have lost their Faith in the Universe to support them, and therefore they think erroneously that God has forsaken them. They have adopted bad methods that cater to their needs. They fear change and people who look and feel differently from them because they fear they will be 'taken over.' Hu-mans have lost the art of hearing and knowing their God. They feel totally isolated and alone, and they feel the need to control every portion of their lives. That is why All That Is created Dog to help return Hu-mans to a State of Grace with their God."

I lean against my angel and pant hard. "This is so much to take in all at once. Am I right to think that I was fearful and not hateful when I attacked Hazz, and that Hazz was full of fear and not hatred?"

"Hazz has been in every Life with you thus far, and he remains a Hu-man in great pain. His continual actions, in each Life, prove that what he does not understand he fears. You said it yourself: what Hu-mans don't understand, they destroy. Over and over, his ignorance has torn him apart and hardened him more. He fears everything, therefore he feels he has to be bigger, stronger, and more in control in order to survive. He believes that a soft Heart will kill him on the spot."

I scratch my head, but not to rid myself of fleas. "So Hazz keeps having bad experiences because he does bad things all the time?"

"Yes, but only for now. As you know all too well, good people suffer because of the bad actions of others. However, those Souls who have a difficult time in Life can be healed and made positive again by the thoughts and actions of other Souls more Enlightened with Grace."

"In the meantime, maybe the Universe will punish him for his bad actions," I say with hope, which is quickly dashed by Azul.

"No, Puck, there is never punishment per se. The Universe is non-judgmental. It is a mirror that gives back what you put into it until a change comes from another. If your reflection is ugly, ugliness will follow you. If you are beautiful in thought, you walk in beauty. If you think you are poor, sick, rich, or healthy, those thoughts will become your reality. Poverty exists, fear exists, sickness exists; all because collective thoughts create those situations. Thoughts create reality. That is Universal Law. All That Is provides the tools to get back into the Heart of Love, which is the true essence of All That Is. This is why Dog has such an important role in Life."

I sit quietly and digest the information Azul has shared with me before I say, "So Hazz is hurting terribly inside. He's afraid to be gentle. He's afraid of loving, and he's afraid of being loved because he thinks—if he does open to the Goodness of Life—he will lose control and won't know who he is."

This heavy conversation exhausts me, and I put my head in Azul's lap. Even though I'm drifting off to sleep, I can sense her smiling.

9

When my eyes opened for the first time, I found myself in a darkened setting, with a lot of warm, snoozing puppies all around me. We were in a small room, and inside a cardboard box lined with a plaid blanket. I sensed I was somehow different from in my past Lives, yet when I looked at my tiny siblings I didn't put two and two together. It was only after I felt my face with a paw that I figured it out. Oh, no, I had no nose!

I got to my feet and balanced myself on wobbly, chubby little legs. I was a fraction of my normal size from past incarnations. My body was fat and round, and I had tiny flaps for ears. Was this a joke, Azul?

My eyes had gotten used to the dull light, and I could now see my littermates clearly. My siblings all looked like piglets. In a high squeaky voice I called out to Azul, which apparently startled the others, as in short order they were all awake.

Most often, Dog is just born and fits right in with the flow of Life on Earth. But sometimes Dog can remember the past and will question everything about his new Life. This was one of those times, as I had no idea who or what I was supposed to be in my current state of Dog.

"What?" one of my siblings asked me, probably because of the look of surprise on my face.

"What do you mean 'what'?"

"What's wrong with you?" The small black little face that was as flat as a river stone was chiding me.

"I used to be Puck. Yes, Dog with a proper nose and long legs, even as a puppy! I must be in the wrong incarnation. I think I'm a little pig and not Dog." I was beginning to shake.

My tiny sibling laughed and said, "You must have slept all through the whelping and Life orientation. You're certainly not a pig! You're a pug."

"A pug? Is a pug a member of Dog as a species?"

"If you mean, 'Are we Dog, as created by The Most High?' then yes, you are correct, my sister."

"Oh, my, I'm a female too?"

"From my observation, I would say so. Is this your first time as a female? Have you never had puppies in your past Lives?"

I frowned. "No, I . . ." The thought gave me pause. I had a lot to assess. Usually, Azul provided an idea of what was to come before I entered into a new Life. This Life, however, was a surprise in every respect. I hoped she was enjoying the aggravation I was enduring.

"I'm hungry, let's call Mama," my sibling announced rather loudly. All the puppies started yapping in a deafening din, but I was hungry too, so I joined the chorus.

Mama pug stepped into our cardboard enclosure, and each of us scrambled to a "feeding station" for dinner. I drank in her sweet, warm milk, and memories of The Bridge faded away—along with my concerns about what I had become or what lay in store for me this time around on Earth.

I soon learned that we were being kept in what was called a "closet," by a female Hu-man whose name was Sally. My littermates came to adore her, and I as well, although I was certain she was not my Minnie. When she came into the room we tripped over her feet for attention. Sometimes she'd lie on the floor with us, and we'd crawl all over her and give her kisses.

It seemed that all the other puppies were quite adept at controlling their little pug bodies. I, on the other hand, had major problems maneuvering the short round casing in which I was now stuck. When I got old enough to eat table scraps, I often fell headfirst into my food because I thought my nose was well out front of my mouth and would stop me. Once I nearly drowned in the water dish because I submerged my whole body in an attempt to drink and had a terrible time climbing out. And when I tried to run, I generally bounced around like a ball because of my stubby legs. This Life was good, though. We had many things to play with, and the people who came to visit us were always happy and carefree.

Soon, however, some of my siblings started to leave and not come back. I could only assume that Hu-mans had taken them to what would be their new homes on Earth. It seemed that all of us would have a Hu-man of our own, and it wasn't long before only three of us remained. I wondered how long it would be before my Minnie would find me.

But no one came for me, and some nights I thought that perhaps she wouldn't find me at all. Instead, maybe Hazz would be the one to show up at the door and seal my fate in this Life! My Heart beat fast when I had these thoughts, and I trembled.

Sally called out and flung open the closet door. The three of us who remained tumbled out as we always did, barking and wriggling our backsides as our way of displaying welcome. Oh, did I mention I had no tail? Another insult to my memory of being a "normal" member of Dog.

Sally's voice chirped to a female Hu-man standing next to her, "Wilhelmina Overstreet, pick out your birthday present!"

What I sensed now was unmistakable! Finally, she was here! My Minnie! I barked and hopped in a crazy circle. She was as beautiful as I remembered her to be; her green eyes shining bright as ever and long brown hair brushing her shoulders. Yes, my Minnie! She has come for me!

My Minnie looked of us, smiled, then tilted her head toward Sally before uttering the unbelievable: "Oh, no, girlfriend, I can't keep a dog in my apartment. You know that. And even if I could, I have finals coming up, so I have to avoid diversions. A dog is definitely not in the cards. But these puppies *are* cute." She sat on the floor and began petting us.

I dashed into her lap, flipping over in the process, trying to communicate, "Minnie, it's me! It's Puck! You know it's me! I'm yours! Take me!"

"Oh, my goodness," Minnie said. "This one is beside herself." My Hu-man laughed. "She's also pretty uncoordinated, isn't she?"

"That puppy is hilarious. And clumsy is an understatement. She's just too funny to watch sometimes. She's smart, though. Already house-broken. But she doesn't like men. She seems afraid of them for some reason. Odd, since she's definitely never been mistreated by a man in this house." Sally bent down and gave me a pet. "But one thing's for sure."

"What's that?"

"She's crazy over you!"

"Well, she'd better find someone else to be crazy over. I know you want me to have this puppy, but I just can't right now. I'll graduate from medical school in a couple of months . . . hopefully." She rolled her eyes. "And then I go to Memphis to work." Minnie took me in her arms and peered into my glassy little eyes. "I have to admit, she is simply adorable."

"Yes! It *is* me, Minnie! I'm your Puck. You know me! I love you so!"

I had hardly finished my pleading thoughts when she set me aside and picked up a male sibling, saying, "I like this one too. What a cute face."

I went into another spinning circle. "No, Minnie! *Pick me! Pick me!*"

"Thanks for the offer, Sally," Minnie said as she set my brother on the floor and got to her feet. "But you'll find homes for them, I know. Who can resist pug puppies, even that little misfit there." She pointed at me with a finger that felt more like a dagger aimed at my Heart. "Come on, girl. You can buy me a birthday drink instead."

I was both frantic and stunned. The breath went out of me. Minnie *must* have felt our connection. Even if she couldn't have remembered me from our past Lives, she must have sensed me on some level. Regardless, the truth was, she had left! I cried all night, and I got no relief from Azul.

The next day, my remaining brother and my sister were chosen together, and now I was alone with my mother Dog from this Life, who assured me repeatedly that another Hu-man was coming for me. She understood that I'd missed my connection with Minnie, and she was sorry. She also told me that she, herself, had picked the puppies in the litter I was in so that each of us could assume our part in The Plan.

She licked my flat face and told me not to lose Faith, and although she didn't know why my Minnie went off without me, there must have been a good reason. She told me that there were never any mistakes in The Plan; that I needed to hold steady for The Highest Good.

Another week went by before someone chose me. I was certain this Hu-man was not my Minnie; her name was Judy, and she was so excited to have me that I felt good for the first time in a long while.

My new home was exciting, and I was allowed to run from room to room. I felt very important. Maybe this was another Hu-man I was sent to Earth to teach and learn from. Maybe Azul had given me two Hu-mans to unconditionally Love and serve. Perhaps this was why Minnie hadn't chosen me. Yes, that must be it! The real Plan was Judy! That night I snuggled with Judy and gave her lots of kisses, which made her laugh and she told me she loved me.

For the first few weeks of that summer I was the center of attention. Judy had a bunch of great friends come over. We would go off on picnics and everyone played with me. I also loved the soft summer evenings when Judy would take me for long walks in the park across from where we lived.

The one unfortunate aspect of our relationship was that nothing happened when I tried talking to her in thoughts. If I couldn't communicate with her, how was I going to teach her the ways of Dog? I considered that perhaps her "hearing me" would come in time. But for now it seemed that all she ever wanted to do was show me off, as if I were some kind of prize. This was okay with me because the important thing was that I'd won her Heart.

Soon, however, our walks became shorter and she didn't cuddle with me as often. And sometimes Judy got very angry with me for reasons I didn't understand. For example, I was playing with one of her sweaters and accidently chewed a little hole in it, and she screamed at me. Then there was her shoe, which I mistook for a toy and pulled it apart. Judy shouted so harshly at me that I had to slink away from her hurtful words. Worst of all, not long ago she kicked me down the cellar steps because I'd relieved myself on the kitchen floor instead of going outside. I couldn't help myself, as she'd left me in the house by myself for a very long time.

I thought she understood that I needed time to learn about her. Just as bad, I wasn't sure what she was teaching me in return. I felt terrible that I was letting her down—and that I was letting myself down as both a teacher and a student. If she would just listen to what I was trying to tell her!

I asked Judy time and again to let herself go and have fun; not to miss the opportunity to be happy. But she slapped me down whenever I jumped on her to give her loving. We had been happy and carefree, and now I no longer interested her. It felt as though I wasn't in this Life at all; it was an empty world for me.

The silence in the house where I now lived was uncomfortable and sometimes even unbearable. First thing every morning I got to go outside on a chain, but I wasn't allowed to sniff around and take my time. All day long I stayed in the kitchen, mostly in my little bed by the stove, and always alone and not allowed any toys. I spent my time staring at walls of little white doors that never opened, and the floor tended to be cold. Judy fed me once a day, which wasn't enough for a growing pup like me. To make matters worse, the food was hard and tasteless and made my stomach hurt. Often I ran out of water.

Judy was always in a rush when she came home. I'd eagerly run to her and jump as high as my little legs would allow in hope that she'd take me in her arms, but she'd tell me to get away from her and to be quiet. She'd take me outside on the chain and haul me back indoors the moment I finished my business. Afterwards she'd scurry around before leaving again, and I'd soon be staring at the same little white doors, which is why I slept most of the time. I lost my appetite and was losing weight from my already small body.

Judy was doing the best she could in this Life, but she was placing lots of pressure on herself. She talked about working two jobs, and she was seeking a permanent mate. Sometimes, she went on short trips with a male friend. I never got to go with her and was often left alone for days at a time. I was forced to relieve myself on pieces of paper that Judy had left for me to use, yet she was always annoyed when she had to pick up after me after she returned. I was very confused.

The nights when a male friend came over, I did my best to make him happy. I was so grateful for the company, but it didn't last long. He came into the kitchen and said hello but then went down the hallway to what was called a "bedroom," where he and Judy would laugh and talk and make loud noises, always without me. Whenever a male left through the kitchen door, I never got so much as a backward glance.

I didn't know why I was in this Life, and I just wanted to go Home. Where are you, Azul? What purpose can I possibly serve in this Life? Dog was put on Earth to Love and Comfort and Protect—to bring Joy and Hope and Faith. I was failing miserably, and dying of loneliness in the process. I was no longer Dog. Everything I stood for and everything The Earth Mother could provide for me were gone. I slept fitfully, most often consumed by nightmares about Hazz. Why had Azul forsaken me? I understood for the first time what hopelessness feels like.

Just when I thought things couldn't get any worse, they did. Judy came home, acting distant and angry. She stormed around and talked about some Hu-man called a "landlord," and how my barking was forcing her to look for a place to live somewhere else. I hardly ever barked, but she'd begun leaving me chained to a post outside during the day when she went to work, even when it was cold or raining. I had to tell her I needed to come inside.

Today, because she was so upset, I tried to do everything I could to bring her Happiness, Hope, and Comfort. She either didn't see what I was offering or didn't want any of my gifts. She wrapped me in a towel and took me in her car to a building containing Hu-mans I sensed were very sad but who smiled through their pain. They rustled papers and removed my collar, which they replaced with a thin chain that had a small tag with a number on it.

Two thick metal doors swung open, and I heard the most awful howling. I struggled to get away. This caused Judy to cry. She looked at me with watery eyes and said she was sorry. She spun around so fast that she almost fell. She quickly walked off, and I whined after her so show how sorry I was, promising to be good from now on. But, as was the case of late, she didn't hear me. I watched her stumble through the doorway from which we'd entered. My only thought was that I must be brave for her, since her Heart was obviously hurting because I'd disappointed her so thoroughly.

The Hu-mans around me tried to be nice, but I could sense that their Hearts were clouded and annoyed. Maybe they were angry with me too. A Hu-man wearing heavy gloves picked me up and we went through the heavy doors. For a moment I thought this Hu-man was Hazz, and I tried with all my might to free myself of his hold. But I was much too small to have any effect on this person.

I was placed in a small wire enclosure. The floor was damp with something foul-smelling and sticky. Instinct told me not to lick it, and its odor was so strong that it stung my nose. My Heart was beating as if it wanted to break free from my body. Dog of all breeds were in cages everywhere that I could see. And many more I couldn't see I could hear. They asked their angels for a passage Home. I, too, wanted to go Home, and I whined loudly to Azul. Yet no matter the strength or length of my effort to elicit a reply, there was no response from my angel, and I couldn't figure out why she wouldn't she answer me.

I lay down on the cold cement floor, placed my head between my paws, and wept. Azul had told me that the Universe didn't punish; that all Dog needs were always met; that everything fit together for The Highest Good. She was wrong! There was no goodness here! And I had failed being Dog. Minnie didn't want me, and I had disappointed Judy and made her discard me like a piece of trash.

I began to doubt that I'd ever see the sweet Summerland of Home again. I started to chew on my paws in hope of making them bleed. Maybe if I chewed hard and long enough, the blood would flow and wash this Life away. But I fell asleep and awaked the next morning as someone came for me and gave me a bath.

The warm sudsy water smelled nice. A machine blew hot air on me, and when I was dry I felt Divine, the overall experience like The Earth Mother's most fragrant kiss. It gave me so much pleasure to be this clean.

I was taken to another room, and a Hu-man talked about doing something that would take away my gift for having puppies—forever. How could Hu-mans do that? The Earth Mother provides for all animals. She decides who will continue a species, not Hu-mans. Before I could think about this further, a mask was placed over my nose and mouth and I blessedly drifted off.

10

zul appeared to me, but I was not at The Bridge. I was so miserable I didn't even acknowledge her presence. I had no spirit left as she spoke the words of The Law of Francis and the Law of Dog, her voice like tinkling bells. My angel showed me a symbol of a circle and reminded me that all things were connected in perfect Balance. Then her image faded away.

I woke in such pain that I couldn't move. Yet as groggy as I was, I smelled death all around me, and I heard Dog brothers and sisters begging for release. I closed my eyes and hoped that sleep would deliver me Home. If there was an All That Is, if Azul was real and not imagined, please, then, let my wish be granted!

"Puck . . . Puck is that you?" I heard a voice I recognized, followed by, "Can you hear me? Wake up!" I opened my eyes. Surely, I wasn't Home, since my body was still in pain, and I was thirsty and very weak. My eyes followed to the fuzzy Dog shadow that stood outside the chain door to my cage. This Dog was held on a leash by a male Hu-man who was talking to another of his kind. I heard the voice again: "Puck . . . it's me! Now . . . you must wake up!"

I had no energy, or the will to keep communicating, but I managed to ask, "Seeba? Is that really you?" The shadow nodded. "What are you doing here?"

"It's more like, what are *you* doing here? I run the streets as the type of Dog that Hu-mans refer to as 'feral,' so I've been here many times. But you, Puck, how did you get here?" Seeba gave me an odd look and laughed. "And just what kind of Dog *are* you?"

I focused my eyes until I could make out that this Dog was, indeed, my sister, Seeba. Her mere presence provided me with a glimmer of Hope.

"Seeba," I whispered. "I'm dying, but Azul won't take me Home. Seeba . . . Minnie didn't want me." I was in so much pain that every word I formed hurt.

"No, you're not dying, Puck," she said with a little annoyance in her tone. "You've just had 'The Operation.' We've all had it performed on us in here. It's called 'spay' for females and 'neuter' for males. It makes it easier for Hu-mans to control us, as our natural instinct to mate is eliminated. You'll be fine in a day or two."

"What is this place?" I asked, not really caring one way or the other.

"We're in what's called a 'shelter.' We're put here until some Hu-man can come by and adopt us and provide a real home . . . we hope. I've been adopted three times. I'm a very pretty Siberian Husky in this Life, or so Hu-mans tell me. But I love to roam free, and I'm so good at getting away that I'm called an 'escape artist.' " Seeba laughed but became serious and inched closer to the chain door to my cage, "Puck, there's always the chance no one will adopt us, and since I have this reputation for running away, this might keep me from ever being adopted again. The two of us need to get out of here."

"I'm too weak to even think about fleeing."

"You will have to muster the strength. If Dog is not adopted, the Hu-mans send us Home. But it's not part of our real Plan and when we reach The Bridge in this way it causes much confusion. So, again, we need to get out of here."

"I don't think I have a Plan," I said to Seeba and whimpered.

"Do not despair, dear Soul. I have faith in The Plan for both of us. I know how to get out of here, and right now it's our Plan to be together in the exercise yard. Freedom awaits!" She paused and gave me another of her odd looks. "As I'm thinking about it, you're so small, maybe these Hu-mans will put you with only Dog your size. What did you say you were?"

"I didn't say. But I'm a pug. I'm a Dog breed called a pug, and I'm a female."

"I can sense your gender. But a . . . pug? I don't believe I've ever seen a pug Dog before." Seeba gave me still another of *her* looks. "You have no nose, you know? No tail, either? And you carry a constant worried look on your tiny wrinkled black face." She chuckled, "You appear as if you constantly need to be sitting on a silk pillow or on someone's bed." She turned somber. "I'm sorry you missed Minnie." Before I could reply, the Hu-man yanked the leash around Seeba's neck and she was led away. A door creaked open and clanged shut farther down the aisle from my cage.

For the first time in a long while I felt Hope, as Faith in something greater going on around me meant everything to me now. Seeba had reminded me of The Plan. I rested my eyes and remembered Azul coming to me in a dream, the circle symbol she'd displayed, and The Law of Dog. I closed my eyes and, even in great pain, fell asleep.

Seeba was right about my recovering from the operation, because in a few days it was all but a memory. Having Seeba close by inspired me to regain my health in this Life. I ate all of what was put in my bowl and began communicating with Dog around me. I constantly reminded them that they were still Dog. I could sense I was helping my kind cope.

Hu-mans came and went all day. Some smiled and pointed at me, but all moved on to other cages. I was reminded how The Plan united Dog with Hu-mans. Some Dog were first-timers, waiting for what would become their forever Hu-man students. Others jumped for joy when their beloved Hu-mans, whom they'd known from past Lives, claimed them as their own.

In a few instances, Dog in this shelter had no Plan involving a single Hu-man. These Dog had sacrificed to bring light to many hard lives before finding a way to the shelter. These Dog had instilled compassion in Hu-man Hearts. Theirs was a noble Lifetime; one that was highly honored at The Bridge.

One morning I was led outside to a large barren patch of ground, separated by chain fences, called an "exercise yard." There was little of The Earth Mother in this setting, but Her sun shining on my face was Divine, and I drew in long deep breaths. The Earth Mother's clean air in my lungs reminded me that She still sustained me, even in this often terrifying place where I now stayed.

To my great joy I spotted Seeba, who'd been placed in an enclosure next to mine. I yelped at her as she jumped around and barked to express her delight at seeing me.

When all Hu-mans had left us alone, she told me to check around the corners of the pens to see if I was small enough to squeeze through the gaps between the fences. At first I thought I could fit through, but the actual size and shape of my body didn't allow my escape.

Seeba let out a sharp bark. She went over to the corner of her pen and poked her nose at the iron bars on a grate. She clawed at its lower section until I saw it pull up a bit and fall back when she released pressure. I think she'd done this many times before, as she seemed pleased with her herself as she pranced to the opposite end of her enclosure. She smiled at me as they led her back inside. No doubt, whatever The Plan had in store for me, it was about to begin.

━ ━

Several straight days of rain had kept us from the exercise yard. During this time many Dog were led from our large cages and new Dog brought in to replace those taken away. I never again saw those Dog who'd left, and I assumed they were sent Home by the Hu-mans. Very sad.

The rain ended, and a Hu-man I'd come to know led me outdoors. I was delighted to be placed in the same enclosure that Seeba had occupied the first time we'd met outside. I waited for her at the door of the enclosure but she never appeared. I paced the hard ground and peered through the fence to see if she might be in a different pen, but Seeba wasn't here. Since I also couldn't smell her scent, my Heart sank. But perhaps she'd been adopted again. Yes, that must be it! It would be impossible for Dog as friendly and beautiful as Seeba not to find a home on Earth.

The Plan had unfolded for her but not for me! I was overwhelmed by the feeling of isolation, and I started howling into what was damp afternoon air. Any hope of escaping with Seeba was now gone. Seeba had found a loving home. No one wanted a chubby, funny-looking little dog like me.

I'm not sure how much time had passed, but all the other Dog had been put back in their cages and were now eating, and I was the only one left in the exercise yard. The Hu-mans here had forgotten me as well! My Heart broke under the weight of this latest in my series of abandonments. I was unwanted and ignored by all the Hu-mans who'd selected my littermates over me, and I was passed on by Minnie to become an unloved burden for Judy, who dumped me here like rubbish. And now my only hope, Seeba, was adopted and happy someplace far away from me. I didn't even try to bark an alert to anyone that I'd been left outside. Instead, I curled up by the door of the building, where I whimpered and closed my eyes.

"Seeba . . . you're here!" I shouted as the sun's rays hit my face. However, when I sprang up to see her, I found that I was still in the exercise yard. It had been nothing but a dream, so I slunk back to where I'd planted myself.

It was then that I heard, "It's no dream, my good friend." Seeba sidled close to me. I circled her and yipped and leaped for joy.

"Hush, Puck, and settle down. You have to do exactly as I say. We haven't much time."

"But . . . how did you get here? I thought you were adopted?"

"No, my luck ran out. The Hu-mans sent me Home a couple of Earth days ago. It's all fine for me, but my departure left the Hu-mans who work here very sad. I was their favorite visitor at this place. They really do have a hard time sending us Home. They want all homeless Dog to be adopted. These Hu-mans' Hearts are truly pure of Spirit."

"I don't understand. If you're Home, what are you doing back here?"

"Azul sent me, but we must hurry, so come quickly and follow me." Seeba led me to the grate that I'd watched her loosen. She motioned with her paw. "Flip that open. It should pop up without too much effort on your part. It's to a drain pipe you can follow out to the street—and to your freedom. Believe me, I know. It's how I escaped every time I was in here, and the Hu-mans never figured it out. I'd do this for you, but I'm in my 'light body' and won't be much help no matter how hard I might push or pull."

I gave it all the strength I had in me, but my effort was to no avail. I whined in exhaustion and sat back on my small haunches. "I have no nose, as you well know, so I can't move it with my head. I can't even budge it with my paws." I growled in despair. "That grate weighs more than I do! I can't do this! I'm just too little!"

Sheba snapped at me, "This is the only way out. Azul sent me here to show you The Plan you need to follow. So keep at it."

I grabbed a flange in my teeth, biting it as well as I could. Nothing! I clawed at it. Nothing! I tried with all my strength to push it even a little bit. Nothing!

I fell back again and whined to Seeba, "Just go Home. It's obvious I can't do this. Maybe some Hu-man will come and adopt me. Maybe that's The Plan. Whatever it is, I can't do this."

Seeba stood over me, glowering. "Puck, you *must* do this. I'm responsible for making sure you begin your Plan. So try again. I'll do what I can to help, but it won't be much with this 'light body' I now possess."

We both pushed, and as I was about to collapse from fatigue the grate slid just far enough for me to wriggle through the gap. I crawled along before I fell down a hole and landed in leaves and mud. I got my bearings and moved to a clear opening—to discover I was in front of a wide street with two lanes of traffic moving both ways.

I didn't know what to do, when I heard Seeba's voice urging me on: "Run, Puck! You must cross to the other side of this street! Go now!"

I couldn't believe what her voice was asking me to do. Obviously this was all Azul's idea. "There's no way I can get across," I told her. "I'm way too little and much too slow. I'm free now, thanks to you and Azul, so I'll just wander around until The Plan shows me what to do."

An image of Seeba appeared in front of me, her fangs bared. "Puck if you don't cross the street right now, I'll bite you hard on the butt to make sure you get going!"

I wailed my objections and backed away. "If Azul wanted me to die and come Home, why didn't she just leave me in the shelter and the Humans would have sent me back anyway? This doesn't make sense. I can't even see the other side of the street. Why do I have to do this?"

"Because it *is* The Plan for you!" Seeba's ghostly image jumped on me. "And it's *my* Plan that I assist you! So get going!"

I started onto the street. Traffic roared by so fast that the draft from the vehicles stopped me cold at times. I waited for an opening and begged for Azul to take me quickly. Soon I was running as fast as my short little legs would carry me. Unfortunately, cars and trucks of all types were quickly on me, and I had to dodge and weave my way. However, I miraculously made it halfway and my confidence improved that I might indeed make it across both dual lanes of roadway.

I waited for a car to pass before advancing and waiting for another to pass. As I pressed onward, tires squealed and brakes locked, but the opposite side of the street was getting closer and closer. I was almost there, and I focused on where the concrete ended and the green grass awaited. A car zoomed by, and I made what I believed would be my last move. I would be correct; I never saw the truck.

— —

I didn't wake up in the soft lap of Azul. Instead, I was on a warm pad in a shiny cage with all sorts of tubes connected to me. The pain was palpable, but my feeling was that it would be far worse if not for something which flowed through my veins and made me woozy.

I was alive, but I didn't understand why. I had said that time didn't exist for us, either on Earth or at Home, but on Earth I could attest that the "now" was the present. And when that "now" moment was full of agony, it did seem to last forever. And then I saw what I was "now." I had lost two legs: the right front and the rear left; so I had one leg on each side of my body.

Apparently the Hu-man who'd hit me with his pickup was so upset and guilt-ridden that he insisted I not be "put to sleep," which is another way of saying he would not send me Home. He'd told the animal healers, called "veterinarians," to save my Life no matter what it required. Since this Life had lost its meaning for me, I didn't care.

The man who'd run over me was a doctor, and he now stopped by often to check on me. His name was John Callahan. He was a big man with a merry way of talking, and when he laughed it seemed no one could resist laughing with him. When he picked me up I felt secure because his hands were so huge. I sensed his Heart was very good, too, and he wanted me to respond to him. For now, however, I seemed to be half in my body and half outside, and I didn't want to be loved again—only to be abandoned once more.

The Hu-mans in this "veterinary hospital" were very nice, and they did their best to make me happy. In return I did what I could to show my gratitude and respond to their desires. Every morning someone held me in a standing position so I could balance on my two legs. However, whenever I tried to move forward, as they wanted, I fell down. I didn't understand what they were expecting from me and growled my frustration.

After a couple of weeks of my stumbling around, a Hu-man fashioned two sticks into tiny legs. This Hu-man strapped them onto the stumps where my own legs used to be. Over and over this Hu-man tried to get me to walk naturally with these things attached to me. The sessions were long and quite painful. My Heart wasn't in this at all, and I failed miserably at trying to walk with these "prostheses," as they were called.

Although the Hu-mans who worked at this place gave me their support and affection, it all meant nothing to me. I chewed ferociously and relentlessly on the fake legs to show my disapproval. But to make certain I couldn't continue gnawing on them, a hard circular thing was placed over my head and around my neck so I couldn't reach the stick legs with my teeth.

So all I did was lie around and do nothing. What could I do with that thing around my neck that made everything so difficult? I even stopped eating. The Hu-mans did get me to drink from a bottle with a metal straw in it, but I hated "eating" like this. Confused and desperate to be free of anything that had to do with this stupid little body I was left with—now not even whole—I whimpered every night for Azul to take me Home.

— —

One afternoon, John Callahan came by and announced that I would be going off with him. Everyone hugged and kissed me as he whisked me away from the cold, steely place that smelled of medicine and had been my home for how long I didn't know. He took off the hard, stiff collar I'd been wearing and unbuckled my stick legs and stuffed me under his coat.

John propped me up in his lap as he seemed to fly down the road in his pickup. He rolled down the window and the fresh air on my face reminded me of Home. I got sentimental and whined a little. He stroked my head and told me that everything would be better from now on. I didn't know what to think, but the air on my face at that moment felt wonderful.

He pulled his truck into a big cement parking lot with cars and trucks in spaces marked by numbers. He placed me under his coat as he strode toward an enormous building. We weaved our way down long hallways while he said hello to practically everyone he came into contact with. These Hu-mans all seemed to know him well, and they acknowledged his greeting with a smile or a wave or a welcome of their own.

We arrived through heavy doors that sprang open by themselves, letting us pass through as if they knew we were coming. Quietly, John came up behind a woman and kissed the back of her neck. She squealed with surprise and spun around to face him.

"Here, Sweetheart," John announced. "If anyone can work miracles with this sort of thing, it's you. I figured she would fit right in around here and maybe offer a little moral support once you work your magic on her." John laughed loud and happy, something I'd learn he did with ease.

The woman gasped when she saw me. "Oh, my God, John! Is this the little dog that ran out in front of you last month? She's precious!"

"Well, she's yours now. She wasn't making much progress at the vet's. It's like her Heart and Spirit were broken, and since you're the best rehabilitation nurse I know, happy birthday, Minnie, my Love." Minnie. The name rested in my mind for a moment. Minnie. These two Hu-mans kissed each other with me pressed between them.

I peeked around the room to find it filled with broken Hu-mans. They all looked like me: missing arms, legs, sometime both or all. I sensed Hu-mans with no dreams, no Hope or Faith of returning to those things that had given them joy in the past. I started to shiver, not because I was cold but because of excitement. I now had the opportunity to teach, to Love, to share what I knew about abandonment, abuse, hopelessness—when it hit me: Minnie! The reality swept over me, and I don't know how I did it but I launched myself from John's arms and into hers!

"Minnie! Oh, Minnie! It's me! Your beloved Puck! Remember me? Puck!" My Hu-man and I were finally reunited! John's guffaw echoed off the walls as Minnie could hardly contain me in her arms as I wriggled.

"Oh, my goodness!" John said, grinning from ear to ear. "This little dog hasn't acted anything like this before."

"Well, she certainly seems to like me," Minnie said and giggled and held me close. I was delirious with joy. I couldn't give her enough kisses. She lowered me to the floor to let me balance myself on my two good stubby legs. I squirmed around so much, trying to wag my tail that didn't exist, that a few men standing nearby on crutches laughed at me. Minnie held out her arms to me. I had to remember what they'd taught me at the veterinary hospital. Yes, I must do this right for a change!

I wobbled, swaying to regain my balance. I pushed off with my hind leg and hopped forward on my front, bouncing back and forth until I reached her. I must have done okay because John roared his approval and Minnie picked me up and squeezed me so hard I thought I would pop.

"Well, I'll be damned!" a man with a deep voice said from his wheelchair. "Look at that, will you!"

"And you take note, Randy McGee," Minnie said to him and smiled wide. "If this little pug can do it, so can you!" And to me, Minnie said, "What a little imp you are. I'm think I'm going to call you Puck!"

Ah, yes, my Minnie remembered my name!

John produced the two little stick legs and their attachments. He said sternly, "Now . . . ah, Puck, if you can bobble along on those two legs of yours, just think what you can do on four! I don't want you to chew 'em up first. I expect you to learn how to use these and get along at being who you really are!"

And so, I finally understood The Plan; my Plan and Sally's and Judy's and Seeba's and Minnie's and John's Plan, all interwoven together as Azul had explained to me: "All things are connected."

I found myself back being Dog again, with everything now clear: that I was to be "me," regardless of whether I had two good legs or four; that I still had to learn and teach; and that I was, and always would be, complete—regardless of what Life threw my way. And forevermore I would honor The Plan set out for me.

11

*I*t amazed me that this Life of mine could change so dramatically, yet, in its way, no different from the brightest sunlight peeking through the darkest storm clouds.

My new home was something called a "ranch," which was located outside the city where John and Minnie lived as mates. John raised cattle that were kind and intelligent. I'd come across cattle in past lives, but nothing as wonderful as these creatures. Their Plan was to serve The Earth Mother through grazing and fertilizing Her soil so plants could grow more abundantly and healthier. In the end, these cattle would even offer their bodies to Hu-mans for food.

In the mornings, when the sun had just risen, I would bob along with John to say hello to the cattle before "we" went off to work. These fine animals told me that they were both pleased and honored to comply with all Hu-man needs. What noble beasts, indeed!

John was a special kind of doctor called a "surgeon." He put damaged Hu-man bodies back together again. Minnie also worked at the same hospital for Hu-mans, and she made the bodies that John fixed work again. I, as Dog, gave Hope and inspired Hu-mans to use the gifts that John and Millie gave them.

It was seldom easy because many of the Hu-mans who were learning to live again were also hurt in their Hearts and minds. I was told that there were other healers in this place who helped mend Spirits and minds. The goal was to get these repaired Hu-mans back into the outside world and functioning right along with those of their kind who had never been damaged.

Minnie explained to me this was a place for only those Hu-mans who were warriors. They had been injured fighting other Hu-mans who wanted to take things away, or to protect those who were being overrun by others. I remembered wars going on between tribes when I was Here before. Wars affected everyone involved, no matter how righteous the reason for the conflict. Sometimes, for those Hu-man warriors who managed to survive, the injuries were impossible to repair. And some Hu-mans suffered who didn't actively fight in the wars. For all these reasons our jobs were very important, and I was so very grateful to All That Is for providing me the Honor of serving these Hu-mans, and for bringing me back into Minnie's Heart.

"I swear, this little dog knows exactly what I'm thinking," Minnie told John on the way to work one day as we rode in his truck, which he called "new and expensive." Minnie wasn't too impressed by it, but John said he loved it. And he loved my Minnie almost as much as I loved her, so I told her this in my thoughts.

"She loves me," Minnie said. "It feels as though we've known each other forever. I can't thank you enough for bringing her into our lives. What she's doing for my patients is miraculous. They see her courage and how she lives in the moment. It's as if she's telling them, 'So what if you have only one leg? Just get up and use your good one! It's no big deal. You're still you.'"

John chuckled and scratched my head as we waited patiently for an event called "a light to change."

Minnie said, "You won't believe this, but yesterday Puck brought a marking pen over to Cory Jenkins, the paraplegic I told you about. Puck jumped up on his chest and dropped it, as if to say, 'Here, write something; draw a picture.' So we started him on using his mouth to create art and to communicate his feelings." Minnie laughed and stroked my fur. "She's such a little scamp. Now she flies up and down the corridors as if there was nothing wrong with her —and there isn't, according to her actions. She's an inspiration for anyone trying out a new prosthetic device. I know she still would rather bob along as she does at home, but she seems to know how important it is for her to show those wrestling with new legs and arms that they can do it. She's my amazing little professor."

"I didn't at first, but now I really like the name you gave her," John said. "Where did you come up with it, anyway?"

Minnie raised her eyebrows. "That's the name she told me belongs to her." She laughed. "I'm joking, of course, but it's the name of that mischievous sprite, Robin Goodfellow, in 'A Midsummer's Night Dream.' It fits her, don't you think; a mischievous, opinionated elf?"

"Well, she *is* that, my love." He squeezed Minnie's hand and smiled. "Ah . . . just like someone else I know."

I smiled, too, hearing my own name in the same Life. I had been named many things from Life to Life, but only one name was really "me"; the name that was given to me at Creation. It was the name Azul called me by; the name by which I was known at The Bridge: Puck. Minnie had many names throughout my Lives as well, but they all came back as *her*. As Azul said, all things are connected in one way or another.

I had complete freedom to come and go as I pleased when we were in the place called a "ward." Being I was so little, I was also allowed to sit on the beds beside Hu-mans referred to as "patients," and I curled up on their laps when I felt it was appropriate. These patients listened carefully to what I was telling them about Hope and overcoming their discomfort by filling their waking moments with action and purpose. Most Hu-mans wanted to work through the conditions they now found themselves in, and I was always eager to help.

Some patients, however, closed up like the leaves of a prayer plant when I came around, as if they were comfortable in their own darkness. They didn't want anything gentle around them, or to learn to move forward. They didn't want anything to upset the dire straits their Hearts were in. It was easy not to be bothered by feeling better, since that would require forgetting the past—and to them their past defined them. The common thread that bound every one of these patients was the fear of becoming whole again. They sadly believed that they had been reborn into this new person; a Hu-man who had survived a horrible experience from which a return to any sort of normalcy was impossible.

So, I sat for many Earth hours with these sad Hu-mans and listened to their woes. In return, I spoke my thoughts to them. It didn't matter if they understood me right away or not. They would get it eventually. I told these Hu-mans with broken Spirits that I knew what it was like to feel abandonment, to lose all Hope of better outcomes, and how it felt to not want to live any longer. I truly understood their feelings—all too well.

Minnie used me as an example of what could be accomplished by living in the "now." She was an intuitive healer, and we worked well in that regard. She read my thoughts and relayed them to her patients. She made them think positively. She taught them to forgive their bodies for not working the way they would like, and she showed them how to resolve the situation that had torn them apart. She made them understand that Love is what really matters, just as Dog knows that Love is All That Is.

As for me, I was able to do everything a "whole" dog could do. I ran and jumped and played fetch with the patients until they tuckered out, not me. I could play for hours. Happiness did that; made you want to play forever. And at night I often slept in the same bed with John and Minnie, in the same peaceful way I did in Azul's lap.

At work today I played fetch with Arnold, who had lost both his arms and was learning to throw and catch a ball with his feet. He did pretty well even though his aim didn't always match where he was looking. His last "toss" rolled beyond the big heavy doors to the ward just as an "attendant" came in. I barely got clear of the doors before they shut behind me.

I was never supposed to be outside the ward, but here I stood with my little red ball in my mouth, wondering what to do. Minnie didn't know I was out here, and I didn't think Arnold saw where the ball went, so I did as all Dog would do: I went exploring.

There weren't many Hu-mans in these hallways, and I bobbed along unnoticed by doctors and nurses, all of them walking and reading at the same time. No one looked down and caught sight of me as I made my way through a maze of corridors. Some of the patients I walked past sat motionless in wheelchairs and stared as if at nothing. I sensed they weren't in their bodies. Something terrible must have happened that made them not want to think—or feel. Why some Hu-mans were given this Life to live out didn't make sense to me. I would have to ask Azul.

I was hopelessly lost now, so I slowed down and peeked into every room I passed. I still had my red ball, just in case someone needed a smile, but it appeared everyone here was either so very angry or so extremely hurt that there wasn't much chance of my making a difference with just one quick visit.

Then I passed a room that stopped my little feet in their tracks. Oh, no! The smell of that most evil Hu-man! The hair prickled across my back and my mouth became dry. He was here! Hazz, the Hu-man I'd killed; Henry, the Hu-man who'd killed Mitchell; the horrible Hu-man so steeped in fear that his hatred had created a circle of pain in Life after Life!

I glanced into his room and took a step inside, every instinct telling me to run away, but for a reason I didn't understand I kept walking forward.

Henry was a gigantic man, dressed in orange pajamas and sitting in a wheelchair, looking out a window. He was bound in an upright position to the wheelchair, which was much sturdier than all others I'd seen. He glowered as if expecting me. How could he know I was here? I was just a little pug Dog, and I'd lost two legs. Did he possibly remember me as wild Dog, who'd torn out his throat many Lives ago?

I arrived in front of him, holding my little ball in my mouth, and studied him. I'd seen his restraints, which I recognized from seeing other patients wearing them, so I understood he couldn't reach out to kill me. I sat quietly and tried to touch him with my good front paw. He responded with a sour smile. My Heart was beating incredibly fast as I called out to Azul for help. I didn't see or hear her, but I felt her Peace and believed that she was with me.

This Hu-man filled me with loathsome fear, and feelings of hate rose inside me for what he'd done to Mitchell. I was asking Azul how to deal with this hate when I saw Hazz as a small child, living back on the Flats where I had met Mia so many years ago.

His mother loved him even though his legs were crippled from birth. She nurtured him, and he thrived in her Love and trusted care. But his mother's mate, who was not Hazz's real father, took him from their village and left him far away from their tribe. Hazz remembered watching his mother turn away and offer no protest as he was carried into the brush. Abandoned and alone, fearful of the animals who waited to satisfy their hunger, the toddler couldn't understand why his mother no longer loved him.

Hazz was found by a nomadic female Hu-man, who raised him but beat him and abused him so badly that he took his anger and grief out on any living thing he could destroy. He learned to walk, and he created havoc wherever he went. He hated female Hu-mans, and he despised seeing living things thrive in their beauty. He lived in constant fear of never being worthy of Divine Love.

Azul had told me at The Bridge: "He's afraid to be gentle; he's afraid to Love; he's afraid of being loved because he believes that if he opens himself to the goodness of Life, he will lose control and won't know who he is."

Remembering her words, I stepped right up to Hazz, and in one mighty leap for Dog my size, I landed on his thigh and let the ball fall from my mouth and onto his lap. I communicated with him in my way: "I understand you now. I see you as good and beautiful. I'm sorry I took your Life once, and I forgive you for creating all these Lifetimes of pain for others. I'm sad that you took Mitchell's Life, but I know that everything is somehow connected. I want you to know that I Love you, unconditionally. I see you, Hazz, for what you really are, and I forgive you."

In one swift movement a huge hand was around my throat and squeezing the Life out of me. My little red ball bounced across the floor and rolled into the hallway. It would be useless for me to struggle, and I'd be Home in Azul's arms anyway. Yet even with the Life being squeezed out of me, I forced through my last breaths, "I accept you, Hazz, as a Divine spark of The Most High that is one with all of us. I am in you and you are in me, as we are all in the rocks, the trees, and every blade of grass. We all fight some kind of battle on this classroom called Earth, and you have a choice to live longer in your Hell or to turn yourself into the Light of Love. Yes, you can be afraid for many more Lifetimes. But eventually you will be consumed by the Love that resides in all things, and you will recognize who you are. You have the choice to let the Light of Forgiveness enter you right now, for I have forgiven you. I love you, Hazz . . . love you . . ."

I relaxed into the flow that would take me to The Bridge, my two real paws now soft on his arm, my eyes lovingly on his. I thought of Minnie and John. I would miss finishing this Life with them.

"There!" I heard Minnie scream, followed by squeaky rubber shoes scurrying on the tile floor. "There's Puck's ball! Oh, my God, no! Puck's in with Harvey Stills! Oh, dear God . . . no . . ."

I never took my eyes away from Hazz's. I was dizzy, passing out, when his powerful hand slowly released me. I didn't jump off his lap or flee. In reality, I couldn't. But when my breathing improved, instead of flopping off him, I licked his hand and jumped up and licked his chin. His eyes brimmed with tears, and he buried his face in the fur on my back and sobbed, his terrible odor gone!

Minnie spoke softly and carefully lowered herself into a chair near Hazz, whom she referred to as "Harvey." She was crying as she reached out to touch his hand. Another caregiver, a Hu-man male almost as big as Harvey, patted the shoulders of the evil Soul I'd feared for so long and said to him, "Everything is all right now."

Minnie lifted me away from Harvey and held me close as I kissed away her grateful tears. She got up to leave just as John came running into the room, his generally pleasant features showing great strain. He folded Minnie and me into his arms and whispered, "Thank God."

Out in the corridor, doctors and nurses and other staff buzzed around as if a celebration was going on. I heard them talk about a "breakthrough," a welcoming back of a lost Soul. Everyone was petting me and saying, "Bless you." I must have done a very good thing for them. I know it was sure good for me.

12

Every Thursday I was taken to visit Harvey, who, according to the caregivers at the hospital, had lost his mind when he fought in the Afghanistan War. They said he'd been silent and unresponsive since he was transferred to the hospital years ago; that the horrors of war and his depression over living this Life in a wheelchair had taken their toll.

He was paralyzed from the waist down and had been combative whenever anyone offered help. Harvey tended to be so violent that he'd been considered untreatable. But since my visit, according to Minnie, he had agreed to seek rehabilitation in her ward. She told me it was because I lived there, which made me jump for joy.

I've changed also since my visit with Harvey. I can't really describe how I am now, except for maybe being more peaceful inside, happier than I ever imagined possible. It was almost as if I was already Home at The Bridge, even though I was still Here on Earth.

I saw things more clearly now, too; how suffering was necessary for growth to occur, and that not a single Soul would ever be lost when on the Path to become one with All That Is, who always provided everything needed to come Home. Dog, Hu-man, whatever, just had to follow The

Plan given to each of us, because we were all connected in some way. And Dog was placed on The Earth Mother to help piece the puzzle together.

— ⁓

Minnie and John were going to a faraway place. Which of course meant me too! There was a lot of talk about people in "Africa" who needed healing and food that The Earth Mother couldn't provide enough of because Hu-mans had wasted so much of Her gifts. We were going to help balance The Earth Mother, just like the old days for me.

At our last day of work at the hospital, everyone threw us a big party. It was like going Home to The Bridge except it was here in the hospital and people were saying goodbye instead of hello. Our patients were sad to see us leave, and I got lots of teary hugs and kisses from the many Souls who lived in the "now" thanks to me and Minnie. Harvey even wished me a tearful goodbye, as he'd also begun talking because of my Love for him.

On the way out into the parking lot, Minnie and I passed a big yellow Labrador being walked into the hospital with a funny-looking harness strapped to her back. She carried an important swagger about her and wore a vest with the words "Service Dog" written on it in big bold black letters. Our eyes met and we instantly recognized each other.

"Seeba!" I yipped, and Minnie stopped so I could "investigate" the other Dog.

"Puck! What are you doing here! Oh, I know! The Plan! It must have worked out for you!" The Hu-man walking Seeba stopped and my sister continued, "My goodness, you have only two legs! A pug with two legs! I've seen everything now!" Seeba laughed. "I see this doesn't bother you much. I imagine you'll have quite a story to tell me when we meet again at The Bridge."

"Oh, yes, I will." I jumped up and licked her face. "I would have never found my Minnie if you hadn't forced me to cross the street. Without your *prodding*, I would never have experienced the beautiful Life I now enjoy. But, I must ask, what are *you* doing here of all places?"

Seeba smiled and continued on with the person holding onto the harness. Over her shoulder, she called back to me, "I've graduated, Puck. I'm here to teach and serve *my* Hu-man now. My Hu-man's name is Harvey Stills. I'm trained to do all the things he can't do for himself, and of course teach him how to think like Dog. He'll be mine for many Lives! Wish me luck!"

My Heart swelled with pride as I watched my wonderful sibling go up the steps and through the hospital doorway. Minnie tugged on my lead to get my attention and said, "Someone you know, huh?" I panted my "Yes."

We were lifted into The Father Sky by a big silver metal birdlike thing and taken to a hot and very dry place. It was the Flats where I'd first met Mia! Once we'd settled in a thatched hut, Minnie said to John," Oh, my gosh. I just had a feeling of déjà vu."

John doffed the wide straw hat he was wearing toward my Minnie. "A lot of people have that same feeling about Africa. They say that this continent is the seat of all mankind. Could be you were a Shaman, way back when."

I smiled at what Seeba had told me at The Bridge, that my Mia had become a holy woman, a healer, a seer, and a Shaman.

We traveled in a vehicle called a "Jeep," stopping close to the camp where I had tried to rescue Mia when I was wild Dog; yes, where I had killed Hazz. The tribe living here was poor and starving. Sickness hung in the air like the still breath of an impending storm. Other doctors and nurses had arrived here ahead of us, and they greeted us with much enthusiasm. I spent most of my time getting used to new scents by visiting everyone and everything.

Minnie delivered vaccines and other medicines that we'd brought with us, and John began treating the locals. In the early evening, the tribal leaders took John out to evaluate the dry, sandy land where nothing of edible value currently grew.

I hopped around with John and sat beside him as he crouched down to let the arid earth run through his fingers. He told the village

Hu-mans, "Years ago, this land was fertile and grazed upon by animals who kept The Balance. This livestock was killed off, and now there's not even enough food for small game. We'll irrigate the land so that water runs through here as it did a thousand years ago. We'll sow seeds. We'll bring in cattle and goats to graze on new grasses and in turn fertilize the soil. Small game will come back to the area, and predators will keep the dance of Life correctly in line. The Earth Mother is forgiving, and in time She will supply you with all that you need to survive. But for this to happen we must help reestablish The Balance."

I smiled at John. He knew much. Minnie had found the perfect mate. They were both profound healers, they knew the power of "now," and they fully understood unconditional Love. Minnie spoke to the women about The Universal Law: "Everything is at your disposal to bring Hope, health, and a better Life to you and your people. Your thoughts form your actions, so let us all imagine a better village and create it now. Hold your babies close and envision perfect Love, which is truly All That Is."

I was so proud of her. She had learned the lessons I had taught her to perfection. She glowed with The Light of The Most High, a level of beauty that took my breath away.

In just a year of Earth time there was joy in the village with much singing and dancing. Water flowed in irrigation ditches, and The Earth Mother had produced as promised. Some noble beasts had begun roaming the land once more, giving and taking in perfect Balance. And I, well . . . I was ready to go Home again, but this time it was different because my task as Dog was completed.

On this night, the sky had so many stars that it looked like a satin shawl salted with sparkles of light. The land was beautiful, with moonlight shadowing the living beings that moved slowly across the Flats. In the distance, I heard Dog howling to All That Is to question its role in this Life. The Earth Mother whispered back through Her breezes, "Trust me."

I was tired and hobbled over to the hut where Minnie and John slept, each mate tangled around the other. I sat peacefully, hearing them breathing calmly. I thought about how beautiful this Life had become. Yet could it have been this perfect without all the pain and fear and death and sorrow that had preceded it? No, I decided. The darkness and the storms were vital to what would evolve into Peace and Light.

I lay down against Minnie's back, just as I did a thousand years ago when I took her for my own, and exhaled into Spirit.

I have my legs back, as well as a handsome nose and a long tail, and I feel wonderful! I take off running and yelping happily across a deep green carpet of grass, tearing into the shallow brook I know so well, sending diamondlike droplets merrily into the bright clear air. I'm Home! But where is Azul? Will my angel be pleased with me and look forward to my next Life?

I race through The Summerland, imagining myself as a silver comet. I start spinning around and around. How good it feels to be whole and complete once more! However, my great enthusiasm is halted when I come upon a Bridge much different from the one I'm familiar with. This one is brilliantly infused by golden rays of Light. Every living thing created by All That Is seems to be standing silently nearby and watching . . . me!

I of course have no idea what this is all about, when I see Azul. She's dressed in a white dazzling gown of Light and motions me to come to her. I approach her with some trepidation. Usually a party is waiting for those who come across The Bridge. But this isn't The Bridge we all use, and it's now made of pure Light in the colors of a spectacular rainbow, arcing up and over to what or where I cannot begin to guess.

Azul's face is so bright that I cannot judge her disposition, but when I come close to her she bows her head, her arms spreading wide to honor me. All of creation bows down in front of me . . . me . . . Puck, who is Dog! I take a step back, not sure of what this means and how to address such a sight.

Off to my side stands The Holy One, whom we know as Francis. He approaches me and touches my head. Immediately I hear his voice lovingly reciting His Rules. I'm transformed into angelic energy and my Dog body disappears and I become dazzling Light. Azul looks up at me and smiles. I ask her in a naïve whisper, "Azul, am I . . . *you*?"

"In a sense, dear Puck, but you will go even further than I. You have learned and taught the most poignant lessons of The Most High; that of Forgiveness and unconditional Love, in the way only Dog can teach Hu-mans. You are no longer Dog, as you now take your place in the Heart of All That Is to be free to enter all Hearts at all times to instill the gift of Love. You are now Love in the purest form. We honor you."

All around me the most beautiful music begins playing. I'm over-whelmed with the exquisite beauty of the melody. Yet as flattered as I am by all the attention I'm being given, and hardly understanding any of it, I must ask Azul: "What about Minnie? I miss her already. Will I miss her forever? I love her so much, and I'm not sure I want to be an angel without her. She might need me again, and I won't be there for her. She loves me!"

Azul smiles and nods, "Puck, do you not know that Hu-mans have their own Bridge called Heaven? When they have achieved all their Earthly missions and learned The Laws of Dog, Divine Love brings them also into the Heart of their All That Is, which they call God. Then, in perfect timing, they meet their beloved Dog teachers at The Rainbow Bridge, to be reunited forever in Eternal Grace." She smiles and sweeps her arm toward The Bridge.

I walk up and across its high arcing span. Every step infuses me with what I am now: Pure Love. I recognize Minnie immediately, and she swirls around me in a celestial hug. I'm delighted to know Minnie is still my Minnie and I'm still Puck, only this time we look different and meld into each other as one.

There is one more lesson that Minnie and I both learn. We discover that there is no rest for Divine Love, which we both are now. We go where we're needed, and we arrive instantly.

Minnie and I enter the Heart of a mother unsure if she wants her newborn baby, and we give her the gift of Maternal Love. We drift into Souls ready to pass into Spirit and show them the beauty of the journey.

We visit families and give Love for one another. We also drop in to see Harvey Stills, and we fill his Heart to overflowing with Love for his faithful service dog, Seeba . . . whom he has named Mitchell. Clearly, all things are connected in some way.

Minnie and I pass over John. He sees us and smiles. We're all together for a moment, but John is told he needs one more Life before becoming one with the Light where we now exist. I assure Minnie that it won't be too long.

I stop by my old Home at The Bridge to see Azul again, but she's busy with a new recruit who appears just as perplexed as I was when I first arrived. Azul knows I'm there because she closes her eyes and presses her hand over her Heart for a moment before continuing to recite The Law of Dog to her impatient student: "Now pay attention, Ginger. You are Dog, the most honorable creation of The Most High, whom we refer to as All That Is, which has made you an instrument of Peace to teach the following:

> Where there is hatred, we sow love;
> Where there is injury, pardon;
> Where there is doubt, faith;
> Where there is despair, hope;
> Where there is darkness, light;
> Where there is sadness, joy.
> We ask that we always be reminded not to seek what we give;
> To console as to be consoled;
> To understand as to be understood;
> To love as to be loved;
> For it is in giving that we receive;
> It is in pardoning that we are pardoned;
> It is in dying that we are born to eternal Life.

And remember, Ginger, Love is All That Is."

The End

Made in the USA
Middletown, DE
16 September 2021